Becoming My Mother's Daughter

LIFE WRITING SERIES

In the **Life Writing Series**, Wilfrid Laurier University Press publishes life writing and new life-writing criticism and theory in order to promote autobiographical accounts, diaries, letters, and testimonials written and/or told by women and men whose political, literary, or philosophical purposes are central to their lives. The Series features accounts written in English, or translated into English from French or the languages of the First Nations, or any of the languages of immigration to Canada.

From its inception, **Life Writing** has aimed to foreground the stories of those who may never have imagined themselves as writers or as people with lives worthy of being (re)told. Its readership has expanded to include scholars, youth, and avid general readers both in Canada and abroad. The Series hopes to continue its work as a leading publisher of life writing of all kinds, as an imprint that aims for both broad representation and scholarly excellence, and as a tool for both historical and autobiographical research.

As its mandate stipulates, the Series privileges those individuals and communities whose stories may not, under normal circumstances, find a welcoming home with a publisher. **Life Writing** also publishes original theoretical investigations about life writing, as long as they are not limited to one author or text.

Series Editor
Marlene Kadar
Humanities Division, York University

Manuscripts to be sent to
Lisa Quinn, Acquisitions Editor
Wilfrid Laurier University Press
75 University Avenue West
Waterloo, Ontario, Canada N2L 3C5

Becoming My Mother's Daughter

A Story of Survival and Renewal

ERIKA GOTTLIEB

Wilfrid Laurier University Press

WLU

We acknowledge the support of the Canada Council for the Arts for our publishing program. We acknowledge the financial support of the Government of Canada through the Book Publishing Industry Development Program for our publishing activities.

Library and Archives Canada Cataloguing in Publication

Gottlieb, Erika
    Becoming my mother's daughter : a story of survival and renewal / Erika Gottlieb.

(Life writing series)
ISBN 978-1-55458-030-9

    1. Gottlieb, Erika. 2. Gottlieb, Erika—Family. 3. Gottlieb family. 4. Holocaust, Jewish (1939–1945)—Hungary—Budapest—Personal narratives. 5. Toronto (Ont.)—Biography. 6. Budapest (Hungary)—Biography. 7. Mothers and daughters—Biography. I. Title. II. Series.

FC3097.26.G68A3 2008   971.3'54104092   C2007-906464-7

Cover design by Sandra Friesen. Cover image by Erika Simon Gottlieb: *Recollections: Flight (Those we leave behind)* (oil). Text design by Catharine Bonas-Taylor.

∞
This book is printed on Ancient Forest Friendly paper (100% post-consumer recycled). The paper used in the colour section is approved by the Forest Stewardship Council (FSC).
Printed in Canada

Published by Wilfrid Laurier University Press
Waterloo, Ontario, Canada
www.wlupress.wlu.ca

CONTENTS

v

FOREWORD

E rika Gottlieb has probed the depths of a troubled inheritance and a balancing grace in *Becoming My Mother's Daughter*. Between the ravages of the Holocaust in Budapest, Hungary, where she and her family were born, and the treasures she discovers in her mother's old handbag in Montreal, Canada, Gottlieb's journey traverses lands, languages, and seas in order to declare: I mourn, therefore I am. It is in the mourning, Gottlieb concludes, that her life continues. She uses the allegory of the streetcar and its underground city routes at important intervals in her story: the narrator must choose to climb aboard the streetcar when the conductor beckons her, and on this vehicle she must travel through the tunnels in order to come out the other end. Her journey represents the stages of Eva's becoming Eliza. *Becoming My Mother's Daughter* is truly a story of survival and renewal, but it is also a story of *malaszt*,[1] or grace.

In 1944, death is all around the family and their friends, all around Budapest, a city that lost the majority of its Jewish population in the last few months of the war. As László Karsai tells us, "according to conservative estimates the number of Jews in Hungary on October 15, 1944, was approximately 300,000. Most lived in Budapest, and many were at work in the countryside as forced labor servicemen."[2] Eva and her mother are among the numbers in Budapest, and Eva's father, Stephen, is one of many Jewish Hungarian servicemen forced to work in the labour battalions.

As ruthless as the Nazi invasion of Hungary was, however, the historical details are not Gottlieb's concern. She is more interested in the ramifications of inheriting the trauma suffered in these times, in the psychological and emotional ties that are formed between mothers and daughters in a traumatic circumstance, and in the natural evolution of families and the roles their members take on as they mature and develop. Eva's mother, Eliza, philosophizes about death when her vulnerable daughter is only fourteen years old: "Believe me, dearest, it really is not so horrible to die. It's the way of nature. Once you're ready, it's a grace" (171). Between "nature" and "grace" there are many gradations of love, sorrow, guilt, and shame, all of which are expressed by the narrator as she makes her way through the tunnels, those underground passageways of the psyche that must be traversed above ground. The middle chapters are divided accordingly into the three most significant adjustments of her life: The Tunnel, 1913–1944; The Tunnel, 1944–1945; The Tunnel, 1952–1982. While these divisions are chronological, Gottlieb does her best to interfere with the coherence of such representations of time by using flashbacks and meditations to cut across such historical categories. The tunnels are, after all, symbolic images taken from a poignant dream that repeats itself:

> The dreams often repeat themselves. [Eva] is on the outskirts of a city, where the streets are unknown to her. They form a maze. She has to reach her destination by streetcar, but it is not easy to find this streetcar or to board it. She must squeeze through a tunnel, a series of tunnels, before she can climb on. And then the streetcar itself has to go underground for a long stretch, squeezing through a series of dark tunnels, or several sections of the same tunnel. (18)

We can see the narrative of *Becoming My Mother's Daughter* as "the long stretch" toward a state of being in which the unconscious is brought out into the light, but we can also read the narrative in a phenomenological way as a continuing story of becoming, of reaching toward furtherance and the accumulation of wisdom, provisional though it may be. Eva intuits the task in front of her. To retrieve the pictures of her family's past,

> she will have to go deeper and deeper into that tunnel: the tunnel of the family past has taken her into a tunnel even darker and narrower, to her own childhood, the very centre of her being, the very centre of her ties with her mother. (51)

To move deeper and deeper into that tunnel, Eva must come face to face with the complex phenomenon of mourning. Gottlieb's narrator tells us that Eliza screams unnaturally at her Aunt Rosie, ordering her to simply *stop mourning*. Aunt Rosie replies matter-of-factly: How is one able to stop mourning? This question is much more significant than it appears at first, masking the mother's inability to call her own mourning to a halt in the period of the second tunnel. But it also foreshadows the narrator's respect for and acceptance of the meaning of mourning in life as she passes through the third tunnel. It is in mourning, we suspect, that the narrator finds the power to write, and in mourning that she also finds the grace and wisdom needed to bring the two women back into each other's intimate orbit.

In 1945, as a child of seven, the narrator recalls the repetition of the parental edict—do not mourn—and within it is the hope that the family would survive the trauma that was inflected on the Jews of Budapest when everyone in Europe was already imagining the victory of the Allies. The mother of the family is inclined to focus on the positive, to breathe life into their present and future in spite of what has happened to them. Eliza's solution is the only one within her immediate power: "Mother is intent on giving thanks for our survival," and so she becomes pregnant with a third child. Eva interprets this as an affirmation of life:

> [Eliza] becomes pregnant as a way to thank God for our survival, for bringing back Father, for keeping the four of us alive—our little family. We're not to mourn; the children are not to be reminded of the dead, the losses, the pain and the fear. We're to rejoice. Stop mourning. (124)

When Eva is a teenager and the family has moved to Canada, Eva and Eliza are said to "dream each other's dreams," but it is not long after that Eva begins to separate from Eliza. The reader is waiting for the mourning to surface again, ready and waiting. Eva's resentment toward her mother leaks into her language: "When I grow up, I want to have a place that's simple and spacious, none of these heavy gilded frames that collect so much dust, none of the antique silverware that has to be polished over and over. I want to be free from all this; I don't want to end up a slave like my mother" (139).

Paradoxically, what the daughter comes to resent most is the totality of her mother's dedication to her household, to her children, to their safety. Yet this, too, is an aspect of the narrator's conundrum, another opportunity to mourn the family's past sorrows and embrace the current ones. The narrative ends on this note, expressing symbolically Eva's squeezing through the tunnel (of the birth canal?). She finds herself at the crossroads, reborn, ready to embrace the heavy yellow handbag her mother has so graciously left behind:

To continue her journey, she has to complete a circle and break out of a circle. To find her way out of the maze, she has to enter yet another maze. And it is a frightening, difficult entry she must squeeze through, a tunnel into the belly of a ship, the inside of a streetcar. To continue her journey, she has to find that lost bag, that heavy handbag is like a burden yet also full of gifts, of treasures. (27)

Readers feel graced by this story, both allegorical and historical, both personal and public, both about the living and about the dead, and they feel both the sadness and the joy of the endless circle in which both are so perfectly inscribed. This book is indeed like the "fresh fragrance of rain over summer grass. A landscape in which I can be consoled, calmed, soothed after tears."[3]

Marlene Kadar

Notes

1   The Hungarian word *malaszt* is translated as grace, kindness, and even divine grace. Erika Gottlieb uses the adverb, gracefully, often in the text, to describe bridges and other architectural forms, but she explains that her source for the "archaic" word is the Catholic prayer "Hail Mary, full of grace," where grace is associated with divine purity and motherhood:

> "grace" in Hungarian is malaszt, and I don't quite know why, but this archaic word, which nobody uses anymore, conjures up for me a landscape in diffused light after rain. The fresh fragrance of rain over summer grass. A landscape in which I can be consoled, calmed, soothed after tears. This word, which I don't understand at all, is also, to me, a colour. *Malaszt* is the colour of the transparent celluloid rattle, my only memento from my infancy and a gift from my dead grandmother, something I had to leave behind in my nursery just recently. (53)

2   "The Last Phase of the Hungarian Holocaust: The Szálasi Regime and the Jews," *The Nazis' Last Victims: The Holocaust in Hungary*, ed. Randolph L. Braham with Scott Miller (Detroit: Wayne State University Press, with the U.S. Holocaust Memorial Museum, 1998), p. 105.

3   These words are Gottlieb's and lead her to remember her celluloid rattle, her link to her grandmother and her past. See page 53.

THE BRIDGE

This afternoon Eliza barely has time to greet her daughter, she is so eager to talk. Yet the words come with an effort.

"Do you know, my dear, there is something I've never admitted to anyone to this day, probably not even to myself. I think I really didn't love my mother when I was a child."

There is a pause. Eva brings Eliza's wheelchair to a halt. At the end of the long hospital corridor, with her back to her daughter, Eliza is turned toward the picture window. Yet she seems equally oblivious to the neat rows of attractive townhouses in this well-groomed Toronto suburb and to the rapidly changing lights and colours of the early September sunset.

"Hard as I tried, it was just impossible to love her."

In the corner of the small lounge by the window, Eva pulls up a chair next to her mother's wheelchair:

"You didn't love her? But didn't you say how eagerly you used to wait for her visits when you were boarding in the convent? Or at that horrible woman's, who was looking after you in the countryside when you were little?"

Eliza takes another pause. She answers slowly:

"She was always so strict, so ready to frown, to scold. I must have told you, I even called her 'Aunt Mother.' It's true I was afraid when she wasn't there with me, but I was also afraid when she did appear. Afraid I must have done something wrong and she didn't really want to see me."

"But haven't you told me she would never arrive to see you without big handbags full of food and gifts? That she would always arrive laden with parcels?"

"Yes, yes, no doubt about that. I knew she would arrive bringing me gifts. Yet when she arrived, alone or with my father, her face was set so *hard* ... she had a *frown*. I know now she must have suffered from headaches—she had high blood pressure—but as a young child I thought I must have made her angry."

Eva looks at her mother slumped in her wheelchair. Where is that robust, moon-faced young girl with the Rubenesque body and melancholy eyes Eva remembers from the old portrait that used to hang in their dining room in Budapest? How vivid among Eva's childhood memories is that oil painting of the teenaged Eliza, her glowing skin set off by the dark background, her high colours in contrast to the brooding veiled eyes.

In her late sixties, Eliza is frail, with a slight hunchback, the once glowing skin now the pallor of parchment. Only her gaze is the same, the energy of those deep, powerful eyes that even behind the glasses can turn formidable with hurt or resentment, only to melt the next moment into the warm glow of humour and understanding.

When being taken out to the corridor, Eliza no longer has to wear the shapeless hospital gown tied in the back. To be allowed her own pink flannelette gown, something from home, has been a small victory, a signpost on the hard-won, halting, yet triumphant progress on the way to recovery. And when it comes to mobility, so far she has tried walkers with and without wheels, contraptions with armrests, hand rests, elbow rests, now canes, anything to help her retrain the thin, weak legs that have been out of commission for such a long time—she is radiant with energy. And grit. Sometimes Eva experiences a sinking in her stomach as she watches her mother grab her two canes, ready to start her breathless, erratic march down the corridor, not always able to negotiate the spot where the lifted canes must land.

Eliza is showing the same determination to win back the use of her legs as she did when trying to regain command over the rest of her body, which for four recent interminable weeks, in intensive care after her operation, had been kept alive by a battery of instruments and machines, squads of physicians and nurses. Kept alive, so it seemed to her, with no contribution on her part. Yet, Eva realizes, this must surely have been an illusion. Healthy or ill, Eliza was always strong-willed, refusing to obey any authority but her own, over herself or over those who belonged to her. At ninety pounds and shrunk to the size of a child—she has become smaller than her ten-year-old granddaughter—Eliza still refuses to be babied by Eva. Hovering over Eliza at her towering five foot seven, Eva sees herself turning into an anxious mother who is forced to watch from a distance as her little one makes her own way across a crowded, busy street.

"You're far too anxious about me," says Eliza, breathless amidst the hustle and bustle of her two flailing canes, yet taking obvious pride in her power of self-locomotion. "Stop worrying so much. I'm much stronger than you think and the doctor insists I move about as much as I possibly can."

And move about she does, physically and mentally. She refuses to read the novels her daughters keep bringing her. Although she was a voracious reader when she was younger, she is preoccupied nowadays with the flights of her own imagination.

"Did I tell you, Eva, about the dream I had the first few days after my operation? It's a recurring dream—I'm going round and round on a long winding corridor, trying to find something. There are several people dressed in white cloaks, standing at a long counter, some kind of reception desk. One of these men stands out. He's also dressed in white, like the others, but on his face I see an expression of sympathy and regret. And every time I try to get close to him, he looks at me and shakes his head and says, 'No, no, you must try again, Eliza, you must keep trying.' Then the whole process of turning around, back through the winding corridor, starts again. When I reach him again, I look at him with hope and fear, not being quite clear about what I'm searching for. He looks at me again and slowly, regretfully shakes his head: "This isn't right. You haven't found it yet. You cannot enter the door.'"

Eliza's face is turned toward Eva, her brown eyes clouded by the intensity of the memory.

"I go on, trying again. 'Where did I go wrong?' I ask myself. 'How do I get there? How do I find it? And what is it I'm supposed to find?'

"I think—how should I say it?—somehow I know it's the truth I'm searching for. An answer to some question. Something that would finally give me peace. And I'm being forced to search until I find it. But when I get around the curving corridors, I find myself once more face to face with that man in white at the counter. And he just keeps shaking his head regretfully. Time after time."

Eva senses that she should not interrupt with questions. It takes Eliza all her concentration to describe the breathless, eerie feeling of her dream, yet she is also somehow in command, in control of her memory of it.

"I circle back to my childhood. It must be part of the same dream. Over and over I'm back on Locs Street, in the furniture factory where I lived with Mother when I was thirteen. Life was quite good then. I went to a good school, where I was popular with the other girls, and I was no longer living among strangers. I remember playing 'Für Elise' on the piano in our little apartment in the backyard of the factory, playing the sentimental parts over and over again. I was madly and hopelessly in love with George, a handsome young designer who worked in the factory.

"'When he hears me play the piano with so much feeling,' I imagined, 'how could he keep resisting my feelings for him?'

"I particularly loved a song called 'Ramona.' It was a big hit in the twenties. I kept hammering the tune on the piano, very loud, and singing the lyrics oh so wistfully. Terribly off key, of course; it goes without saying."

They both smile as Eliza pretends to sweep her long, elegant fingers over a keyboard. Eva is quite willing to pursue the lighter tone in Eliza's reminiscences:

"Did the young designer know you were the boss's daughter? Or wasn't your father living with you in the apartment?"

"Well, yes, he always lived with us for a few days of the week, but he also had his own apartment away from us. I remember how nervous he was one day when I decided to surprise him by turning up at the family store uninvited. He made it painfully clear that he hadn't expected me, that he didn't want to be reminded of my existence in public. At least, not just then."

Eliza grows pensive. She has never resolved her feelings for her father. To Eva it has always been hard to reconcile her own memory of her loved and most loving grandfather with the image of Eliza's remote, mysterious father.

Eliza continues, "Yet when I see Father in my dreams, I want to go up to him, to touch him, but it is he who is elusive. I never really resented him. Even when he was in a black mood, I feared him less than I feared Mother. He was a great one for hugs and kisses. When we went for walks, he would take my child's hand in his huge paw. I remember how huge his hand was—mine was lost in it. But I don't think that as a child my mother ever hugged or kissed me. Ever. I just can't remember."

"But surely she must have. When you were ill or hurt? Surely you must remember times when you were ill or unwell and she showed how much she loved you."

"Not really." Eliza raises her eyes to her daughter, who sees the old hurt still unappeased, unanswered. "It's hard to talk about it. Sometimes she was so instinctive, irrational, unpredictable. How clearly I can see her. I can also see myself—I must be seven or eight years old, sitting on my high stool in the dark, dank, cobblestone courtyard outside our one-room apartment on Heart Street. We were trading picture postcards with the other children and we were having a good time, our ears were buzzing with the excitement of deep concentration. I don't remember exactly how it happened, but someone must have bumped into me, or I just suddenly fainted, because I fell off that stool and struck my head on the pavement. I ran crying back to our apartment.

"Mother had been working at the kitchen table by the window, and she must have cut her hand when she saw me fall. Now, as I entered crying, she raised her hand at me with the knife still in it. She was furious:

"'I saw you from the window. Look what you made me do.' I can still feel my shock at her poor bleeding hand, the knife, her rage. I darted out of the apartment and didn't come back until Auntie Helen called me in for supper."

Auntie Helen was Eliza's beloved aunt, Ethel's youngest sister. For a while before they emigrated to South America in the early 1920s, Auntie Helen, her husband, and their two children all lived with Ethel and Eliza in this one-room apartment. Eva knows well all the players in that old family drama. Yet there are always new details, new revelations, in the twists and turns of Eliza's stories.

"Still," Eliza continues, "I identified with Mother very deeply. I knew she had trouble paying the bills, putting together the rent for the first of the month. Seeing her anxious about money, I felt called on to solve her problems. In the way of an eight-year-old, of course. There was a grocery store at the corner. I can still see the big brown barrels standing next to the door, and the big colourful tins on the counter. How clearly I remember the exotic aroma of cocoa and fresh-ground coffee wafting over the pungent, tart odour from the barrels of sauerkraut and garlicky dill pickles.

"In the corner of the shop there was a huge, cast-iron grinder. One day I gathered my courage and asked Mr. Kis, the grocer, to hire me as his assistant. At first he laughed—I was eight years old and quite puny for my age—but then he took me at my word. After school—I was in grade two— I could hardly wait to start. How proudly I took my place at that enormous cast-iron grinder. I'd crank the big, unpainted wooden handle for hours, churning out bags full of almonds, walnuts, poppy seed. I was paid a penny for each order, no matter what the size of the bag. Then, late in the afternoon, I would run home to Mother to show her my earnings:

"Look, Mother, I've got twenty pennies here—now you don't have to worry about the rent any more, do you?"

"And what would she say?" Eva prompts gently.

"Oh yes, at times like this she was truly touched. For a while, anyhow. But still, it seems to me, when I was a little girl she never showed me her gentle feelings directly ...

"Of course, you understand, when I look at her through the eyes of an adult, there's no doubt in my mind. Of course she loved me, deeply. But that is not what I felt as a child. Take the time when I was still a boarder in the convent, when I was six. This was right after the Great War, in 1919, during the occupation of the city by the Romanians. With the other girls in the convent, I watched the soldiers from the window. They wore black uniforms. They marched in a solid black block. We were excited. We were afraid. We were also hungry. But the nuns were very strict, and we weren't allowed to complain. I thought of Mother often. The convent was on the Buda side of the river, and Mother lived on the other side, the Pest side. We were separated by the Danube. Her only way to reach me was by crossing the Lanchid, the Chain Bridge.

One day when she was on her way to see me in the convent—she was already on the bridge—the Romanians opened fire with their artillery. She threw herself down, covering her head with her hands and her handbag. She said it simply never occurred to her that she should turn back. Crawling on her stomach, crawling along that long bridge under fire to see me, she just kept on going ... When she reached the convent—it was quite far from the bridge, and the streetcars weren't running, so she had to walk—she was out of breath and still badly shaken. But she smoothed down her long, dark skirt, readjusted her hair, which she wore in a loose chignon around her face, and then triumphantly pulled out a crumpled brown paper bag from deep in her handbag. Her heavy, knitted handbag was covered in dust, completely out of shape, but somehow she'd managed to keep the paper bag intact. And inside it there were three crisp rolls, each one laid thick with butter and a slice of ham on top—worth their weight in gold.

"'Come, come, Eliza.' She grabbed me by the hand.

"Quickly, with a conspirator's glint in her eyes, Mother pulled me along the corridor until we found an empty classroom. She thrust me in ahead of her, then pulled me behind the blackboard, standing guard to cover me from view as best as she could. She could hardly wait for me to eat; she didn't want the nuns to get their hands on those delicious rolls she had found for me. I had no doubt she was as eager as I was. And she

The bridge

absolutely refused to taste them herself. Hovering over me grimly, she watched me devour one roll after another. I started to feel quite heavy with all the food, especially since I didn't dare ask for a drink of water. After I wolfed down the three rolls, I felt duty bound to finish the crumbs at the bottom of the bag, every last one of them. I can still see myself, an always hungry six-year-old, almost choking with greedy delight over this sumptuous undeserved feast. Oh yes, I also remember feeling overwhelmingly grateful to that grim young woman who risked her life to bring me this. I was overwhelmed by gratitude, but I also felt guilty. Guilty for still not being able to love her."

Eliza's eyes grow moist at this recollection. She doesn't want to hold back anything from Eva or from herself. She is searching. Eager to go over this ground even though some of it has been covered before. Somehow the answer to the wordless question asked by the man in the white cloak at the end of the winding corridor hinges on her feelings for her parents, especially her mother.

"I keep going back to Heart Street, to Locs Street, then to our lovely house where I got married when I was nineteen, to all the different places, all the different homes I shared with Mother. The answer is somewhere there, I know. Yet I don't quite know how to phrase the question."

As Eliza nears the end of her story, she becomes aware of the view, the impressive row of stark-white townhouses backlit by the sunset. For a while mother and daughter sit quietly at the window, their eyes on the glowing, meandering highway that leads to Eliza's current home in Toronto, only a ten-minute drive beyond the hospital and the white townhouses.

The blue streaks in the sky are turning deeper, but the shimmering pink and orange reflections of daylight flare up once more, as if in resistance to the encroaching darkness. Suddenly, in the playful magic of this sunset, Eva observes the familiar white townhouses of suburban Toronto turn into a whitewashed Mediterranean village by the sea, or rather into a seascape out of time and out of place, with the familiar highway transfigured into a bridge gracefully arching over the sea. Then, in that split second when the eye suddenly becomes aware of the pale phosphorescence of the evenly distributed streetlights, the timeless seascape with the never-ending bridge begins slowly to fade away, to dissolve into the darkening blue of the sky. Settled on the edge of the yellow plastic settee next to Eliza's wheelchair, Eva places her hand lightly over her mother's. Except for the slightly protruding blue veins, how transparent her hands have become in her long illness.

"The question, Mother? What else could it be? It must be as you've said before—finding a sense of truth, a sense of peace. Probably what some people call a sense of God."

But Eliza is still searching.

"Yes, yes, you may be right. But somehow it seems to me in my dream that it's something quite definite I'm after. Something quite simple. Like a tap on the shoulder, a touch on the hand—a sign of approval, a kind of agreement, a confirmation ... I don't quite know what."

Eliza's hands rest lightly on the arms of her wheelchair. Her eyes are lost in the soft velvet of the night. Her deep, almost masculine voice has lost little of its resonance even during her long illness. But now it suddenly sounds tired, its modulations reduced almost to a monotone whisper.

"You see, as a child, and even later, as a young girl, I often felt unjustly treated, accused of ingratitude. When I was eighteen I couldn't bear it any more. I ran away from home and returned only after I saw my parents' desperate message in the classified pages of the paper: 'Eliza, come home. Mother is severely ill.'"

"But even after I ran straight home, I felt my parents' silent reproach for not being grateful enough for the sacrifices they'd made for me. Of course they'd made sacrifices—especially Mother. Then why could I not love her in return?"

"It was only after Mother had her first stroke, a few weeks before she passed away, that I realized what she had meant to me. By then it was as if she was no longer my mother but my child, who depended on me, whom I had to teach to walk, to speak. But it was, by then, probably too late for words between us."

In the dark, the white townhouses are sharply illuminated by the streetlights in the foreground, and the long road leading to Eliza's home— the arched bridge over the sea—has vanished. Still turned toward the window, Eliza seems barely to notice. In her dreams and in her waking hours she seems compelled to search for another home, another road, another bridge. She is going back, again and again, to her old homes, the small service apartment in the back of the factory, the even smaller one on Heart Street with the narrow, dank courtyard where when she was eight she first experienced living with her mother. She finds herself back there, wrestling with the same questions. Had she ever had a real home with her mother? Was she ever loved by her?

Had she ever loved her in return?

Suddenly, for the first time this evening, Eliza turns toward Eva and gently takes both her hands:

"It's dark. It must be time for you to leave, Eva dear. I'm afraid I've kept you late again."

Eva glances at her watch without withdrawing her hands. "It's ten to nine. They won't throw me out for another ten minutes yet. You know, Mother, you should try to write down all these things you've told me today. Not everyone has your gift for telling stories. How often have I felt I've been there with you, at Heart Street, in the convent, in the factory, as if I'd lived there *with* you."

Eliza's eyes are tired now. But she looks at her daughter with her impish smile, as if saying, "What a shameless flatterer you can be—don't we both know what we know?" Then she raises her once lovely hands, now gnarled with arthritis:

"Write with *these* hands? I can't even grip a doorknob. Can you imagine how hard it would be to hold a pen?"

Yet having said goodbye to the view from the window, and having been wheeled slowly back to her room, there is no doubt Eliza is excited. Is it the vividness of her words as they bring back old memories of her childhood and her long-dead mother? Or is it the magic of something both Eva and Eliza have suddenly become aware of, that light touch on the hand, that bond, that elusive, precarious bridge that suddenly connects the two of them, another mother and another daughter?

Eva helps Eliza back to bed, then slowly gathers her things from the armchair. The sweater, the purse, the book for the long bus ride.

"You should start writing, Mother. Once you decide to get started, your fingers will just obey. Dearest, it's bound to work ... believe me."

Something in Eva's voice must be contagious, because Eliza's moist brown eyes in her suddenly wrinkled face seem to regain their old spark. But she only smiles her conspirator's smile, as if to say:

"You're only humouring me, but I'll go along as if I truly believed it."

They say goodbye gently. Eliza is suddenly anxious, urging Eva to take a taxi instead of the bus. Eva places her hand on Eliza's high, still smooth forehead, kissing her lightly, saying goodbye. Yet—and this is an old, childish game between them—she only pretends to be leaving. When she reaches the door, she saunters back casually, her eyes sweeping the room as if looking for something forgotten. Casually she walks back to the bed, leaning over her mother. Feigning absent-mindedness, she kisses her goodbye once more and again turns back to the door. Then, with her hand almost on the doorknob, she turns quickly again and saunters back, as if still in search of that forgotten object. By the time they reach their third goodbye, both of them are laughing quietly.

It is with her mother's chuckle in her ears that Eva takes the elevator downstairs, crosses the hall, takes the revolving doors. Yet in spite of her quick steps away from her mother, she feels as if it was unthinkable to tear herself away. And when she reaches the bus stop in front of that solid block of white townhouses under the deep velvet of the September sky, suddenly she feels a tenderness, almost an elation at the pit of her stomach. It is a sensation she could not describe even to herself, like the echo of a burst of laughter one cannot quite repress even on the street or on a bus, even when surrounded by strangers. A short, sharp chuckle as inexplicable and irrepressible as a burp, or a sob, or a cry.

After Eliza's sudden death some six weeks later, Eva sometimes wonders: Was there a reason why Eliza was consistently denied admittance at that door by the man in white standing at the reception desk that marked the end of that maze of endless corridors? Why she was made to return from the door of death after suffering a cardiac arrest the day after her operation? Was there a reason why she had to go through her bitter, pain-filled struggle for recovery when three months after her miraculous return she was cut off so brutally, so abruptly, by a second, fatal heart attack?

Is it possible that that September evening was one of the unfathomable reasons?

But of course, even after the first shock of rage and disbelief was over, Eva would still have trouble explaining what actually happened on that September evening that could have made a difference. Could it have been that on that evening Eliza had found the answer she had been searching for so strenuously while being compelled to circle those endless corridors? Could Eliza finally have found a sense of peace on that evening, simply by being able to ask someone all those questions about herself as a child and about her long-lost mother? How strong the hold of those questions must have been, not letting her go, pulling her back to resurrect the various homes of her childhood, homes long lost on another continent, in a bygone era?

Yet all along, wasn't Eliza letting the real question, the only real one, go unasked? A question beyond houses and homes, beyond all the tragic misunderstandings, all the painful loosening of our bonds with our parents and our children? Hadn't Eliza's groping, troubled questions about her mother received, unexpectedly, some kind of wordless answer in that unexpected moment of tenderness with her own daughter, in that silent, elusive moment of deep understanding between two women pitted against the timeless seascape of that early September sunset?

What else had Eliza been in quest of all along but a sign of approval— a light tap, an elusive touch that like a silent blessing affirms the covenant, the promise of continuity between mothers and daughters? A sign that, at least for one brief moment, the mother's life—her skin, her sight, her hands, her tears, her laugh, the memory in her brain cells—has become part of the daughter's, to be handed down, in due course, to the daughter's daughter. Floating bridges between generation and generation. Bridges over endless dark seas. Where are you leading?

Bridges between mothers and daughters?

Through mothers and daughters?

THE MAZE

"The convent. Has your mother ever told you about the convent?" Eva turns to her niece, Dina, continuing their conversation.

They are sitting on Eva's beige and brown living room sofa, with the other members of the family scattered around the living and dining rooms in various stages of civilized boredom. It is one of those family reunions where, after the elaborate pleasures of the dinner table, the participants realize they have very little left to share with one another.

"These lunches are really getting hard to take," murmurs Ron, Eva's husband, to his eighteen-year-old son, Robbie, as to an accomplice. Although he does not say it out loud, his mischievous grimace indicates that he long ago made a mental note about Eva's reminiscences:

"And now, no doubt, we're in for all those flashbacks—in slow motion, no doubt—to our wartime childhood and the persecution. Strange, a couple of months ago she was incapable of watching a documentary on the Holocaust or even mentioning it in conversation. And now? At any rate, it's time to change the reel."

But instead of interrupting his wife, he turns to his brother-in-law as if oblivious to the other conversations around him.

"Ernie, how about this joke I just picked up at the office. Did you hear the one about the two travelling salesmen ...?"

Ron works in the public relations department of a downtown corporation, a position that Ernie, a mechanical engineer, finds glamorous and exciting for its very lack of clear definition. He receives Ron's efforts at entertainment with an ingratiating smile and a chuckle of anticipation. Ernie's wife, Sandy, turns her attention to the men:

"Quiet, everyone. Ron's telling a joke."

As if giving in reluctantly to popular demand, Ron now says he'll try to tell it, though in this mixed audience he can't guarantee the effect it will have. Ernie receives the off-colour joke in his usual manner, with knee-slapping and appreciative guffaws.

Sandy laughs once, but her laugh ends on a question mark. With her characteristic sincerity she admits right away:

"It sounds funny, but I didn't really get the last line. Could somebody explain it to me?"

With a somewhat regal gesture, Ron turns to Ernie, delegating to him the task of enlightening his wife.

But Dina hasn't yet forgotten what was discussed before.

"Aunt Eva, you started to tell us about the convent. What was it like?"

"What a hypocrite," sighs Robbie, Eva and Ron's eighteen-year-old son. "How she pretends to care when obviously she can barely wait to get away from here."

The gathering's attention, with most of the available passion spent, seems to return to Eva.

"You started to tell us about the convent," Dina says.

Ron jumps up from the sofa.

"Time for another coffee," he announces, then turns to his daughter: "Come, Judy, give your good old daddy a hand. We'll make another pot."

"No, no. Sit down, I'll make it." With a slight tremor of her lips, Eva stands up too.

"I'll tell you about it later, Dina. Unless you want to join me in the kitchen while I'm making coffee."

As always, the family gathering follows roughly the same rituals. This is the time for Sandy to declare peremptorily that no member of her family would ever consider a second cup of coffee, assuming they had already succumbed to the temptation of a first one. Coffee is poison for the heart, for the stomach, for the liver. It is clear that Ernie would love a cup, but after a moment of visible inner struggle, he makes a dismissive gesture as if to say, "It isn't worth the hassle."

By the time Eva returns with the fresh pot, everyone is making to leave.

"But I'll take a cup, since you've already made it, dear," says Ron. "You know I've never refused a cup of coffee in my life."

And in a soft aside for her benefit, he whispers: "And as for intellectual stimulation, this cup of coffee is probably the best thing that happened here all afternoon."

"A ridiculous waste of time," Robbie splutters whenever family gatherings end. Yet the family sometimes needs this common ground, to express approval or disapproval, to test their levels of dislike or apprehension.

They also have a need, which none of them will admit, to honour the memory of Eliza, Sandy and Eva's mother, the four children's grandmother. These family gatherings used to be especially meaningful for her, and the family has kept up the ritual they observed so carefully while she lived. Yet somehow no one talks about her, not even Leslie, her widowed husband. As if it would be bad taste to mention her name, let alone talk about her or admit that they are mourning for her.

Whenever she senses someone is about to touch a dangerous emotional chord, Sandy quickly changes the subject to something she considers more instructive, more educational. Sandy was a science major in her youth, and now, at forty-seven, she is still seeking an empirical formula to eradicate all of life's ailments, all the sadness of the world. Preventive medicine, apple cider, the heavy use of Vaseline, the substitution of Ovaltine for coffee—over the past twenty years, within her family circle, she has explored and zealously advocated a variety of such miraculous shortcuts to everlasting health. The latest of these shortcuts, always combined with whichever trend in pop psychology is current, is supposed to guarantee eternal health and happiness for one and all. In her eyes, not to be happy—that is, not to aim for her most current definition of health, happiness, and good cheer—has always amounted to heresy, or even worse, to bad manners.

These days, Sandy avoids conversational traps—that is, discussions that aren't conducive to health and happiness—by rhapsodizing over a well-furnished or well-designed house she viewed recently in the Toronto suburbs. Ever since her family moved from Montreal to Toronto five years ago, she has been house hunting, and each new campaign she launches emphasizes yet another foolproof strategy for cornering the real estate market and, of course, achieving health and happiness everlasting.

"You've never seen such a charming staircase, and the hanging plants ... If I had any money, that is the house I'd buy. I've just fallen in love with that winding staircase." In Sandy's code, emotions mustn't be suppressed entirely, but they have to be channelled, pruned, trimmed. Like her own healthy houseplants, they must be made to grow in the right direction.

Eva, who has never been particularly successful with houseplants, feels more and more tired and frustrated whenever she cleans up after these family parties. Somehow it is becoming more difficult for her to tolerate Sandy's enthusiasms, to snap back at Ron for his public taunts, to ignore the mild or not so mild jokes he directs at her in front of others, even if she knows why he does it: he does not, he very clearly does *not*, want to be submerged in the past, in emotions. It is, of course, his own past he is resisting, his own memories, his own sense of belonging.

"I'm lucky," he likes to announce. "I don't remember a thing. I have no memory—I've already forgotten everything that happened yesterday. You can test me." Everybody laughs. Yet he refuses to remember only because he dreads to be caught; he refuses to be caught in the ritual of mourning. And Sandy's offensive evasive tactics are also getting more and more difficult to take. Whatever the newest recipe for her elixir of happiness, it always includes a steadfast refusal to return to sentiment, to the memory of their mother, to their common past. Yet since her mother's death, Eva's need to return to the past, to her childhood, has become more than a simple need; it has become a compulsion. Her life is becoming an extended search, circling back time and again, the way Eliza had been circling back in her dreams in her last months to her own childhood. And Eva has kept returning to the most traumatic period of her life, the time when she was six, during the war. The scenes she goes back to are of hunger and cold and terror, of Budapest in the fall and winter of 1944. The taste and smell of iron, blood, and cold on Tatra Street, the horrible laughter and the indifferent shrugs of the gentile strangers around the Jewish women and children made to stand in line in the snow ... Is that line going to be driven to the ghetto or to the Danube today?

Eva had been seven years old when the war ended. She had lived in Budapest another twelve years after that. She had gone to school there, had fallen in love for the first time, had grown up. She had seen the same houses around Tatra Street many times, had seen them under normal, everyday circumstances when going to the store for bread, standing in line for eggs, or simply passing by on her way to school. She had seen the same houses for another twelve long, colourful, variable years—yet the Budapest she was returning to now was the other Budapest that must have lived for her under this normal façade all the time. The city of snow, slush, blood, and hatred. Had these inoffensive grey façades, the six-storey middle-class apartment houses, been there only to cover up the caverns of fear, darkness, and hatred? The houses that had seen the victims driven along the sidewalks in long, meandering rows? The eyes of the buildings had turned inward, blinded to the memory of those inexorable caves, the hollows of memory covered up by the façade of middle-class normalcy in the ensuing years.

Eva found herself returning to that winter almost compulsively, searching for her mother there, as if Eliza had lived for her most vividly, most tangibly, in those months of horror, fear, and homelessness. More vividly than in the memories of long, lazy summers with her on the beach, their hikes in the mountains, or their long walks along the Danube in Eva's early teens. It was when she recalled huddling against her mother's tense, alert body as a frightened six-year-old that Eva felt her presence most vividly.

But obviously, the family was not ready to follow her back to the past in pursuit of Eliza.

"Next time for sure, you have to tell me about the convent, Eva." Dina gives her aunt a big hug as they are saying goodbye. Yet she's never heard the stories from her own mother, Sandy, and has little genuine interest in hearing more about her grandmother's life.

"As for my own children," Eva tells herself as she starts stacking dishes, "they may feel they've already heard too much about the war, the persecution." Judy and Rob are impatient with her stories of the family past. Is it because they really cannot discuss these things with their own friends, because this past makes them feel like outsiders, or is it just that in this instance they've taken their cue from their father?

Eva starts washing the dishes. Ron pops in to make a perfunctory offer to help, but Eva knows that if he did they would inevitably begin a post-mortem of the evening, and she can do without that for now. Tomorrow is Monday. She has an early class in her humanities course, Women and Other Minorities, and she still hasn't assembled her lecture notes.

Eva tells Sandy: "One of these days it would be worthwhile sorting out Mother's apartment and putting her papers and photos in order. We should also get someone to clean the place regularly for Father."

"Oh yes," Sandy replies. "The whole place could do with a cleaning out. We could start by throwing out about eighty percent of what's there. Although I really don't have time at the moment, at least not before I'm finished with our new house."

Once again the family has gathered in Eva's beige and brown living

room. The others have arranged themselves on the U-shaped sofa and on
the hard dining-room chairs the best as
they can.

Robbie is sitting at the dining room
table with his grandfather, their eyes
are riveted to the chessboard. Ron is
watching their game, munching on a
cookie and waiting his turn. Ernie
does not play, but in the chess players' company he feels he can drink his
second cup of coffee relatively safe
from Sandy's scrutiny. Dina is away

Playing chess with Grandpa

at university in Ottawa; her older sister, Clara, has come along to chat
with her young cousin, Judy.

"Look, Clara, let me show you the beads I've just finished making,"
says Judy with all the pride of a ten-year-old. She has brought down her
boxes of colourful bracelets and necklaces and is eager to display them for
her favourite older cousin.

"Which one would you like me to give you for your wedding? It's your
choice. I'd like to see you wear it."

Clara blushes slightly.

"Actually, Judy, I'm not sure I'll have a wedding in Toronto. George and
I are thinking we may just go over to the States." Her voice has risen two
registers.

Judy is disappointed and doesn't know how to hide it.

"You mean I won't be invited to your wedding?"

"Well, Judy, one sometimes has to take things as they come," Clara
tells her, trying to brave out the little girl's disappointment.

"But why would you go to the States? Isn't George Canadian? And
he has his people here, too, doesn't he?"

"Well, Judy," Clara tries to explain, "you see, his family is very, very
different from ours. They probably wouldn't get along very well. I mean,
they simply wouldn't have a lot in common."

Clara is probably right. She and George met at university in their eco-
nomics class. George's father is a judge; his family has a pedigree few can
match in Toronto: third-generation Rosedale. The two families could be
hardly more different, and George's people might well be at a loss with
Clara's—the accents, the different emotional wavelengths, the whole
background ... It's hard to explain to Judy.

"Actually, it's amazing how well Clara got along with George's family," Sandy told Eva after Clara's first invitation to George's home. "And of course George is a very nice young man. Why complicate things with the rest? It's their life, really."

His long, dark hair tied back with a red bandana, Robbie reveals the convoluted logic of his eighteen years as he mumbles under his breath:

"Good riddance, if you ask me. Our Georgie Porgie and his family are a bunch of snobs."

"The wedding? When?" Grandfather looks up from the chessboard. He simply cannot fathom the possibility of there being no family wedding. "But why not a wedding? If his family is here and the girl's also? It's the most natural thing, isn't it?"

"Not really," Robbie tells him. "Unnatural would be for all of us to shake hands with a bunch of snobs."

"What are you saying, Robbie?" Grandfather is getting worked up. "Why don't you speak up? You know I'm hard of hearing. I don't understand a word of what you are saying."

Robbie places his hand gently on his grandfather's.

"Nothing, Grandpa. I just said that they won't get married before graduation. That's almost a whole year from now. I said, 'Let's get on with the game, all right?'"

Eva remembers how glad Eliza would have been to see her oldest grandchild as a bride. In the first few months after her mother's death, Eva has returned to life only gradually. Circling around her, the circumstances of her departure, Eva has spent sleepless nights reliving every bit of action, everything she had done or left undone in Eliza's last hours.

Then after the first few months, the daytime world has resumed its everyday shape, and she has been circling around her only in her dreams. In these recurring dreams, to her astonishment, the mother she believed lost to her is still there. Eva greets her joyously, reaches out for her, talks to her—and then she disappears. Night after night, Eva wanders in a maze trying to find her. She relives her loss again and again.

She goes to sleep expecting to see her again.

The dreams often repeat themselves. She is on the outskirts of a city, where the streets are unknown to her. They form a maze. She has to reach her destination by streetcar, but it is not easy to find this streetcar or to board it. She must squeeze through a tunnel, a series of tunnels, before she can climb on. And then the streetcar itself has to go underground for a long stretch, squeezing through a series of dark tunnels, or several sections of the same tunnel.

Often in these dreams, she finds that she has no money or not the right change for her fare. After the embarrassment of not being able to pay, she realizes she has lost the big handbag she had meant to take on the journey. It is a cheap, quite ugly old bag, but she has valuable things in it. With a child cradled in her arms, she is looking for the bag with a profound sense of loss, knowing she simply cannot go on without it.

"Imagine, Sandy, how Mother would have loved to see Clara in her wedding dress, how happy it would have made her."

Sandy is obviously hurt by the young couple's idea of having no family wedding, the more so since, Eva suspects, it is Clara and not George who frets over who will and who will not "fit in." Yet Sandy will not display in public the unforgivable weakness of being unhappy. To be happy is still a matter of moral obligation for her.

"One can't live in the past, just on emotions," she tells Eva, preparing to launch a lecture. "Sentimentality doesn't help anything. Cut your losses, concentrate on the future. Whatever is best for the children ... You have to face reality."

This has been a hard time for Sandy and Eva. Their relationship has grown strained. To visit their sister Ada in the psychiatric ward, to let her know about their mother's funeral, to look after their widowed father, to think of long-term arrangements for him—these are their issues in common. Yet the only thing Sandy and Eva can ever agree on is that these things form somehow, possibly, a sphere of shared responsibilities. Each approaches every task differently. The two husbands, Ron and Ernie, watch them from a distance, reluctant to interfere. By now, the two sisters' arguments have lost some of their vehemence. Sandy still lives her convictions of the moment, but even these seem to have lost some of their vitality. Instead of sniping at each other, the two sisters keep away from each other, for longer and longer times, each pursuing probably the same solution but according to her own totally different temperament. Somehow, Eva suspects, in spite of the camouflage of toughness, Sandy must be struggling with the same burden of mourning.

While Sandy directs her energies toward renovating and furnishing her new house—her third in four years—Eva approaches reality by a different route. As if reality disappeared and had to be found again.

When Eva saw her sister Ada in the hospital after her most recent breakdown, Ada was unable to accept the fact of death. She was crying, but like a young child, and she kept asking: "But this doesn't mean she won't come back, does it? It can't mean that?"

Somehow, deep down, Eva does not believe in her mother's final and ultimate loss either. The dreams seem to hold out some kind of promise she will get sight of, to reach her mother again. But who is the child Eva cradles in her arms? And what does the streetcar mean, and the frightening tunnels she must crawl through to reach it, and the fare she cannot pay?

And what is her destination on this journey? Somehow, this is the most disquieting of all the questions that recur in her dreams. She is looking for a bridge that will let her break out of the maze.

But what is the maze? And what is the bridge? Somehow she senses that the various dreams connect, like in a puzzle, each flowing from and clarifying the others.

But she is lost when she wakes up and tries to understand what she has dreamed, the same way she is lost in the dream itself, acting out her meandering, leaden journey both when asleep and awake.

Being lost also means being unable, unwilling to go on.

In her dreams the streetcar conductor is looking at her askance. "Do you or don't you want to continue your journey?"

To mourn.

It seems that withdrawing from joy is a means to alleviate the pain. As if by not allowing herself to feel joy, to feel pleasure, the mourner is striking a bargain. As if Eva is cutting her losses by saying, "The loss of life cannot be that unbearable, really. Life holds no pleasure for me to begin with." And there is the bargain. The loss of the loved one can become manageable once the mourner convinces herself that losing her own life would not be such a great loss. Ironically, to survive grief, one must learn to devalue life itself, as one would work on a transaction, a commercial exchange:

"I give up my pleasures so that I won't feel much at all; I withdraw from life itself. And then the pain of loss becomes more bearable."

A bargain. With Nature? With God? With the self?

Eva's children, Ron, her husband, her sister, Sandy, all want to talk her out of that bargain. They seem to be telling her gently but more and more insistently, "Come back, look to the future. One has to stop mourning."

"When will you start painting again, Mom?" asks Robbie, who has shown the most understanding. "Start preparing the next show. You've stopped completely. It's insane."

"You see," Sandy says, picking up an album of family photos Judy has just shown her. "This is a good picture of Mother. She's smiling here. Why don't you paint her portrait from this?"

"But I have never painted from photos. I paint from life, or from the imagination. Which is the memory, really."

Eva is looking around her studio, a small, bright room they've added to the house. The paintings from her last show are piled up facing the wall. Older portraits and landscapes are hanging. But there is no portrait of Eliza.

But Eva remembers with a smile that Eliza used to appropriate all her daughter's portraits. She always had a need to name, explain, interpret Eva's paintings. When Eliza arrived in Montreal in 1958, she saw Eva's first oil portrait, two heads against a red background. It remained her favourite throughout the years.

"*This* is the picture of Sandy and you in the first year," she tells Eva, "when you were all alone in Canada. The picture of homesickness—I recognize you both. Yes, it's that, it must be."

At twenty, Eva does not give a quick answer. In fact, the portrait was her first attempt to paint, at the age of nineteen, that very first dream, the dream of the six-year-old in the ghetto, the dream about separation from those she loved. The tearing away of the ship against a red sky. Although there is no ship in this painting, and the sky you see is only a dab of red paint, the faces show—they have become—the tearing away. There are two faces, one is strong and dark with the curve of thin, determined lips. The other is fair and soft with large, generous lips. Sandy and Eva? Father and Mother? The parable of mourning? The wild, melancholy passionate anger of the darker face; the dreamy, tear-filled grieving of the softer, lighter one. The parable of mourning, of being torn away from those you love, of grieving. A parable of immigration? Saying goodbye to those left behind? (Eva would refer to the picture simply as "two faces"; Eliza insists on naming it "The Homesick." Eva does not argue. In her first Toronto show she gives it the title "Recollections: Farewell.")

Eva's second group portrait is really a triple self-portrait painted in her early thirties. The way the face turns around in front of the mirror, she has titled it "Revolving Mirrors." Again, Eliza wants to see it as some kind of a portrait of her three daughters:

"It should be called 'The Three Sisters,' or if you want to be more mysterious, 'Three Faces.'"

Eva responds somewhat angrily:

The family get-together

"Why do you say that? Can't you see it's a self-portrait? But that really isn't the point—it's a study of the same face turning around in front of the mirror."

She's becoming resentful: "Why does Mother always have to insist on a sentimental interpretation? And why is it that whatever I do, in Mother's eyes it suddenly becomes appropriated by the family, it becomes part of the collective? As if I always have to justify every thought according to the consciousness to be shared by all. Always, always, the family, the tribe. Can I never be permitted to break away, to become nothing but myself?" In another twelve years, in her early forties, Eva has a show of portraits, called "Faces," the show Eliza never saw, the show Eva doesn't dare repeat.

Of course, Eliza has already seen the paintings, in Eva's house. It is at the family party welcoming Eliza home after her long stay in the hospital. It is Eliza's special wish to see them all together at the family table. "Look, Eva, we haven't celebrated Sandy and Ernie's wedding anniversary. And Clara's birthday is coming up soon. Since Sandy is busy with moving to the new house, would you mind hosting the family party this time?"

How lively Eliza is at the gathering. Except for Ada, who had been allowed home from the hospital to visit her mother a week before, the whole family is there. Sandy and Eva with their husbands, Ernie and Ron, and all four grandchildren. For once, Robbie has given up his sixties hippie outfit and, as a great concession to his grandmother, joins them at the table in a clean, untorn shirt. And there are the granddaughters, Dina and Judy, pretty, serene, eager to please Eliza. Clara has brought George, whom Eliza likes very much. Seated next to her husband, Eliza is in her true element, a tiny but powerful matriarch.

She has also brought gifts, joyous wishes, even short, funny poems she has written for her daughter's anniversary and her granddaughter's birthday. Then, at the end of the meal, while looking

Self-portrait of the women in the family

around the room, she notices Eva's paintings, which have just returned from the framing shop in time for the show in early November. Eliza wanders around the room, studying the walls covered by rows and rows of paintings.

"You see, Mother, the idea is to have the same face turn around, to show it from slightly different angles until it turns around completely." Eva is giving her a tour of the twenty-two portraits.

"But didn't you say they were self-portraits?" asks Eliza.

"Yes, you could say that. But the idea is simply to have the same face," Eva tries again.

"Yes, yes, but what I see here is far more interesting. All these faces of you, yourself, Eva—don't you realize they're the faces of our entire family? I see my mother here, and look, this one here looks like Sandy, and this one here is very much like Ada. I see the whole family here— there's my Aunt Helen, and my cousin Esther, the faces of all of us."

"But I ... oh really? It's totally unintentional ... Though it's interesting that *you* say so."

By now Eva is being careful not to argue, not to upset her mother by opposing her. Of course, what she is saying is ludicrous, too far-fetched for words. But if one looked from another perspective, could Eliza have a point, despite Eva's declared intentions?

She's hanging the paintings with Janet, the young, eager curator.

"The intention," Eva explains to her, "is to look at faces the same way we would look at a watercolour landscape—big chunks of colour and the rugged or smooth contours of hills, precipices, caves, covered by the smooth, fuzzy surface of the entire hillside. Yet a landscape that is alive with anger or resentment or wonder. Serene landscapes, troubled landscapes—the landscape of the observing, reflecting human face. The landscape of the human face with the moon craters of memory. The volcanoes of guilt and regret. The fertile fields of regret and guilt transposed; the serenity of love, of survival. By the time the face has turned around completely, there is a complete change of mood and expression."

Janet, the young, eager curator, likes the idea. She likes the paintings. They're excited about the show.

Her last show.

The gallery is spacious and well lit, far grander than Eva had expected. Too grand, in fact. The twenty-two faces should form a full circle, they should fill the room, but they don't. An entire connecting wall between the first and the last portraits has been left empty.

What to do to complete the circle? The "Recollection" pictures, the cycle Eva has been working on since she was nineteen? Or the serene landscapes to show more directly the resemblance between watercolour portraits and watercolour landscapes?

Janet wants something she can live with for the duration of the show. Something she can feast her eyes on. She decides on the landscapes.

It's Janet's decision. Eva agrees.

Yet she feels that the circle has been broken. Or is it simply that it has been left unfinished?

How to complete the circle?

If she wants to have another show here—Janet implies that Eva should have another soon—she should find a way to complete the circle.

Before the opening, Eva tells her mother:

"You're still not quite well, Mother. Maybe you shouldn't come to the opening. It might be quite busy. I may have no time for you. You should come a day or two after."

Eliza does not want to show that she is hurt.

"Don't worry. I'm not well enough to leave the house at the moment."

"But it's only ... Look, we'll see it together on the weekend when you feel better and I can give you all my attention."

But Eliza won't be seeing the show on the weekend. On Saturday Eva is writing the eulogy. The funeral is Sunday.

The show Eva did not go to see after the vernissage.

The show she cannot, she dares not repeat.

Yet deep down, she knows that if she wants to go on, she should complete the circle.

But how to complete it?

Where is the centre? The beginning and the end?

Her dreams ask her the same question.

And her children.

"Mommy, you should stop crying," Judy bursts out angrily. "You shouldn't cry so easily. You never have fun with me anymore."

She is not doing well in school, and she isn't doing much better at home.

"It's boring, it's boring," she says whenever Eva suggests they go for a walk, or talk, or play a game.

It's somehow up to Eva to do something, but she doesn't know what to do. As if they were all asking her the same thing.

"Break out of the circle. Stop the mourning. The year is almost over. Turn back to the present, to the future. Forget about the dead. Forget about the past. Stop mourning."

In the daytime, Eva goes about her chores. By now, her classes take little preparation, but she has to organize her time carefully. She goes to work; she comes home from work. She prepares supper; she asks Judy about her homework; she helps her when necessary; she tries to get through each day.

In her dream, when the streetcar conductor asks her where she is going, she doesn't know.

"Where are you going? Can you pay for the trip? Do you really want to go on with the journey?"

Autumn is followed by a relatively mild but long winter. Spring isn't much better. Eva visits her doctor. Doctor Sol is a serious but rather distant young professional in his mid-thirties. Eva describes her complaints:

"Low energy level, difficulty sleeping—pains in the back, in the stomach, right here in the middle, in the solar plexus."

She tells Doctor Sol that she has lost her mother and cannot get over it. She thinks she needs medical help.

The young doctor is nodding.

"It's all explained then. You're grieving. It takes some time."

"Are you sure, doctor? I've been having these problems for months now. And I have trouble coping at home, and at work."

"Several months, you say? More than three? Has it been more than three?"

"Yes, it's close to nine now."

"Then we can't call it grieving any longer. It's called grieving under three months. After that it's called depression."

Eva and Ron can't help grinning at each other. There's no doubt the doctor is in earnest. He feels he has done Eva a great service with his diagnosis.

In the summer she goes with the same physical problems to another doctor, a woman this time. Her office is on the top floor of a new medical building. Everything in it has the dazzling gleam of white enamel or the sophisticated sheen of stainless steel. She starts by taking down Eva's family history.

"Mother's age?"

"She passed away at sixty-eight."

"Cause of death?"

"She had many illnesses. Cause of death unknown."

The interview is more difficult than she expected. Then the doctor reaches the next category.

"Grandparents. Age of paternal grandmother at death?"

"Seventy."

"Cause of death?"

"She was murdered by the Nazis ... shot in the back of the head."

"Maternal grandfather?"

"Fifty-eight. Also murdered ... by the Nazis."

The appointment is not getting easier for either the doctor or the patient. Eva starts to cry quietly.

The lady doctor peers up through her glasses. The war has been over for forty years. She decides to ignore the patient's reaction.

"Height? Weight?" She goes on with the rest of the questionnaire as if nothing had happened. These are all routine questions. Nothing could have happened, she decides.

But Eva is relieved that the first interview is over. And she knows she will not be going back for a second.

Whatever it is she has to do, she will have to do it herself. To break out of her labyrinth, her prison, her maze. If she could only get back to work. To paint her mother's portrait.

It takes Sandy and Eva almost a year before they can bring themselves to sort out the family letters, the family photographs. Actually, it is Sandy who first takes up the task.

"What I want," she declares, "is to organize them correctly. Then whoever wants to spend time with them, here they are. But first one must always organize."

So it's in Sandy's new house, a spacious bright bungalow with sparkling clean white walls, wide picture windows, light, graceful furniture, and healthy, well-behaved houseplants, that Eva catches sight of those things she must have been looking for all along.

Sandy has methodically sorted through a deep drawerful of Eliza's papers: the pictures in a shoebox arranged according to size; then all the postcards in the next shoebox; and then in the next all the letters, their loose sheets arranged by size and shape, all the boxes like cars on a train, or sections of a streetcar.

"May I take some of these home? Let me just look at a few things quickly—I'll take them home and look at them at leisure. I'll take good care of them. I'll put them into an album."

"Of course, as you like," Sandy consents graciously, with a thin smile of recognition, as if to tell her: "There you go again, creeping back to your little world of the past."

But she offers to find her a big brown envelope, more like a big paper sack, to carry home all her papers, pictures, letters.

Eva stares at the shapeless brown envelope bulging with memories. Her excitement is out of proportion, as if she senses that the envelope may hold her last chance to stop wandering through her life, to find a way out of the maze.

To find her mother once again, the way she really was.

Somehow, she has known all along that her way forward hinges on her painting. She has to complete her circle of portraits. And what is missing from that circle is a portrait of Eliza.

But before she can do anything, what are her dreams telling her? There is something to be done.

To continue her journey, she has to complete a circle and break out of a circle. To find her way out of the maze, she has to enter yet another maze. And it is a frightening, difficult entry she must squeeze through, a tunnel into the belly of a ship, the inside of a streetcar.

To continue her journey, she has to find that lost bag, that heavy handbag that is like a burden yet also full of gifts, of treasures.

Once she knows the streetcar's direction, once she has entered and found her way through the tunnels, once she has found the handbag, she may reach what she's looking for on the other shore; she may find the bridge.

To be able to continue her journey, to complete the circle, to break out of the circle, she must paint her mother's portrait. Since she had failed

Sketches of Mother

to paint it from life, she has to approach it through the imagination, which is another form of memory.

How Eva regrets that she never painted her mother's portrait from life. It isn't that she never tried. Sketches in pencil. Sketches in pen. Sketches in watercolour. "Let me see ... How interesting. This is the way you see me?" Eliza's disappointment is clear from her voice. The wrinkles on her face, the bags under her eyes, the crushed brown velvet of her pupils, the long, bitter lines between nose and mouth, that downward grimace of the full, once sensuous lips.

"Well, if this is the way you see me," she tells Eva with deliberation. "I'm not saying you're wrong, but one sees oneself differently."

Eva's father is a different subject entirely.

"Let me see, let me see," he insists after the first few seconds, before Eva has even established the outlines, the most prominent hills and valleys of the facial landscape. "But why do you say it is not finished already? It's excellent, excellent, first rate."

He probably has no strong need to study his own reflection, though of course he has an overall impression of his own face. Handsome, leonine. "You look like Ben Gurion," strangers often tell him, once they notice his deep-set eyes, the smooth dome of his high forehead, and the crown of wiry white hair.

When Father stands in front of the mirror, he thrusts out his chin; he

Sketches of Father

is politely forceful, like Napoleon surveying his troops for a prosaic, tough everyday world. He sees himself as respectable, reliable, inspiring confidence, poised with determination to fulfill his task. He is not an eye person; he is a task person. The mental task of solving problems in chemical research. Then the family task: Man the provider. Man the protector. Man the providing, nurturing, proud father.

He is always pleased with Eva's portraits of him, and God knows she has made plenty of them. "How did you learn to do it so well, dear girl? It's finished now, isn't it? There, we're all done."

He can barely wait to go for a walk and light a cigar.

"Excellent, my dear, excellent," he exclaims before he even looks at the finished drawing. Then he waves back at her with a smile as he lights up.

Eva's own children are restless when they sit for her. Robbie simply cannot be persuaded to sit down, stay put, co-operate. He warmly recommends that Eva find another, more rewarding model. (She captures his face unbeknownst to him, by the rear-view mirror while sitting behind him in the car.)

Eva's daughter also finds it hard to sit. "I'm bored, Mummy," Judy complains. "I can't sit so long." And when her portrait is ready, she shrugs her shoulders:

"What should I say?"

Sketches of Rob and Judy

Yet whenever visitors look at her framed portrait, she smiles sheepishly.

"That's me, as you may have noticed"

And to her own friends when they enter the house for the first time, she points out with feigned indifference:

"And this is me. My Mom made it. Now let's go up to my room to play."

Eva's husband, Ron, is a surprisingly good model. Unlike Robbie and Judy with their hide-and-seek expression in the elusive, hazy landscapes of childhood and adolescence, Ron has a reliable assemblage of unmistakably mature features and, to top it all, a full, rich beard—a rewarding subject for any painter. And nowadays he no longer complains about the domestic terror of having to sit for her, though he has made it clear that he would never sit without a book in hand. He accepts stoically the hardships of having a wife who is a painter.

Sketch of Ron   A family portrait

"This is still a great deal better," he points out, "than being married, God forbid, to a fellow writer."

In the end he accepts that the portrait is of him. Only rarely does he feel obliged to enter into an ominous in-depth analysis of Eva's troubled subconscious for having presented his nose in an unflattering light. As a rule, he doesn't argue. He rarely shows pleasure or displeasure with his likeness. Deep down, like his father-in-law, he is indifferent to the visual world unless he can make a witty statement about it.

But now Eva regrets having no portrait of Eliza.

"No, Mother, that is *not* how I see you," she should have told her when Eliza was looking at her sketches of an aging, anxious, tired old woman. Because the sketches are fragments. They lack the continuity, the hills and valleys, the many changes yet the unmistakable pattern, the unique texture of her mother's personality. To paint her mother's picture, Eva will need to capture the whole being in all its dimensions. It will have to be a composite portrait, something like a collage, year after year, layer after layer. A portrait in time. A familiar face in the reflection of other familiar faces. The maze of family lives. The tunnel to the family past.

We all live other people's lives.

We all live other people's marriages.

Our parents' marriages we are trying to avoid. To avoid their pitfalls. Yet we often fall into new traps by trying to avoid the old ones.

Because, when we go counter to our parents, who had gone counter to their own parents, aren't we back to the pattern of our grandparents?

The inextricable, fascinating, inexorable patterns of the maze. The maze of family portraits. The dark tunnels of the family past.

THE TUNNEL
1913–1944

Ethel's Photograph, 1913

The first photograph Eva puts in her new album is of a young girl of eighteen. She could be a South American beauty with her round, dark eyes, fine cheekbones, large, sensuous mouth, and shiny dark hair, which she arranges in a loose chignon. Her waist is slim in the white blouse; her rounded hips taper off under the dark, floor-length bell-shaped skirt. The photo must have been taken in the summer of 1913, before the Great War. It is a formal studio portrait of Ethel, Eliza's mother, Eva's grandmother.

Ethel is one of five children in the family of Ignatius Berger, a labourer in the shipyard at Csepel. Eva also inserts here a faded sepia photograph of Ethel's mother, Mrs. Berger—no one alive today remembers her first name. She must be close to seventy in this picture, and she looks remarkably like Eliza looked in her last years. The same wide, generous mouth ready to cry or smile and never, even when smiling, without the deep, bitter crevices at the corners of her mouth. Eva would like to place here a picture of Ignatius, but however hard she tries, she cannot find a picture of him among Eliza's papers.

As the oldest daughter in a working-class family, Ethel has to leave school after grade four. She is not quite twelve when she starts to work for the family firm of the Fehers.

Ethel at 19, 1913

There are also five children in the Feher family: five sons, who work with their father, Sigmund. After his own father's modest beginnings as a small landowner and corn merchant in a town on the Hungarian plains, Sigmund Feher expanded the family corn business and moved to Budapest with his wife, five teenage boys, and impressive capital, just a few years before the end of the old century. By the dawn of the new one, he is the head of a considerable family fortune. It consists of a furniture store downtown, three floors that cater to offices and middle- and upper-middle-class homes, as well as several apartment houses around the city, and later, a factory. With his Hungaricized surname, his portly, dignified bearing and big moustache, Sigmund Feher looks deceptively like his Hungarian gentry neighbours. He also sounds and feels at least as patriotic as them. In his language, his culture, and his strong sense of Hungarian identity, he is far from being an intimidated country Jew steeped in and restrained by the European ghetto tradition.

Sigmund is proud of his social and financial standing. He also sees himself as emphatically different from his city's sizable Jewish working class. (Though they, too, see themselves as Hungarian first and Jewish only second, if at all.)

By the time Ethel Berger finds employment in the Fehers' family business, the five sons are helping their father manage his empire. (Eva remembers seeing portraits of the five tall, robust Feher boys, painted by a fashionable portrait artist of the 1920s. She also remembers vividly Sigmund's formal oil portrait, which used to hang in his oak-panelled office on the main floor of the furniture store. Yet now, when she tries to find a place for Sigmund in the family album, she finds not even one photograph of Sigmund among Eliza's pictures.)

The Fehers are generous and paternal to Ethel. They watch her grow up and develop into a young woman. They promote her several times: store runner, then office assistant, salesperson, buyer. She has a quick, natural intelligence and a good head for business. She quickly learns German, the language of commerce, and she acquires without effort a deep knowledge of the furniture business. When she is eighteen, Stephen, the second of the five Feher boys, falls in love with her.

Stephen's Photograph, 1913

Stephen is six feet tall, brown-haired and blue-eyed, and is considered remarkably handsome. He is also widely acknowledged to have courage, strong values, and a quick temper. Once, when he returned to the office after hours and caught a thief with his hand in the till, he simply walked up to the man and gave him a tremendous slap on the face.

Stephen is twenty-six when he falls in love with eighteen-year-old Ethel. He is also her boss. She trusts him implicitly. At nineteen she becomes pregnant with his child. When Stephen declares his intention to marry her, the Feher family withholds its consent.

"A girl from a big proletarian family?" Sigmund smiles cynically. "You must be out of your mind. Of course, you'll do

Stephen and his officer-brother, Willie, 1916

your duty by the child. That goes without saying. But to allow yourself to be trapped into marrying her? That would mean not only marrying a girl without a dowry, but also accepting the burden of an entire poor family. Her family would surely drag you down, even if she doesn't."

Her pregnancy is a time of shame and humiliation for Ethel. At twenty she finds herself without a job or a home.

"Don't you dare come back here!" Ignatius rages when he learns that his oldest daughter is pregnant and unmarried. "Don't darken my door again. You've brought shame on us all! I've been working for you with all my might all my life, and what do I have to show for it? You've brought shame on your parents, on your sisters. No self-respecting decent person will ever want to look at them after this."

From behind her husband's back, Ethel's mother tries to signal to her:

"Wait for me outside. Don't worry—I'll find a way to take care of everything."

But in front of her husband, even she cannot stand up for a daughter who is no longer respectable.

In the Feher family, no one reproaches Stephen for his lack of discretion. All the Feher boys have love affairs—they are men of the world. Who would frown on young men sowing their wild oats? It is just that the

Fehers would find it unseemly to keep Ethel on staff once she starts show-ing. Stephen's oldest brother, Andrew, makes a suggestion:

"The sensible thing would be to send her abroad before her time comes. Giving birth out of sight may help avoid further shame to her family, not to mention inconvenience to ours."

Ethel is sent abroad. She gives birth to her daughter, Eliza, in Vienna.

Pages from Stephen's Diary, 1916

Baby Eliza is only a few months old when the Great War breaks out. Stephen has been called up as a private. He is the only brother among the five who is not made an officer. Willie is a lieutenant, Emery a captain. Stephen cannot become an officer. Although he completed his courses in high school, he had chosen not to take his final exams. He had typhoid fever in his early teens and has feared ever since that his memory has suffered for it.

Wherever he goes, he carries a small diary with a black cover. He takes notes of everything. Later, Eliza will preserve Stephen's diary, the yel-lowed pages covered with tiny writing in faded ink, the diary he carried with him for all the war years. It covers his years from twenty-eight to thirty-three, which he spent on the front, in the trenches.

Sometimes Eva has to use a magnifying glass to read the writing, as if Stephen were hiding behind the pale, small letters. Yet the writing is clear, evenly formed, almost like print. How well Eva understands, from her own life, the obsession to keep a record and the simultaneous fear that somebody will read it. Tucked in with the diary Eva finds a picture of the youngest brother, Willie, in his lieutenant's uniform. Willie is quite a dandy, elegantly crossing his stockinged legs in his seat, cigarette in hand. The photograph is mounted on a postcard that announces good news: Willie will have a chance to visit Stephen at his regiment.

There are four entries in Stephen's diary recounting the event.

"My younger brother wrote he is coming to visit me. I am excited to see him: I have been on the front for months—we have not seen each other for two years."

"I am thinking of letting Sergeant B. know that my brother Willie is expected to visit me. B. hates me, likes to make fun of me. He knows my family is well-to-do. He hates Jews—he loves to torment me. What will he say when he sees my brother in his lieutenant's uniform?"

"There is no question, B. will taunt me even more after Willie leaves. I am of the same rank as my younger brother's orderly. And I should salute Willie, of course."

"I got another card from my brother Willie. His unit was redirected. He cannot come to visit me. I am sorry—who knows whether I'll see him again? Yet in a way, I must admit, I am also relieved. B. will have no reason to taunt me about the fact that I must be the stupidest person in my family, the only one who will never amount to anything."

Stephen draws well; in his diary he sketches some of the buildings, the architectural details he finds interesting in the different cities where he is stationed. He also has a need to express his emotions in his diary, emotions he cannot share with anyone. His letters to his family are formal, restrained. But in his diary he writes:

"I want to survive this war. It would break my dear mother's heart if she had to lose me."

Wherever Stephen goes, children are drawn to him. He is a natural storyteller, and he invents games and makes toys for them. He makes them laugh with his puns, his word games, his short, terse poems. Yet he believes he has a defective memory, and he feels unworthy of his capable brothers. Though he is the tallest and strongest of them, he never quite feels their equal and he lets them browbeat him. After Sigmund's death, the family fortune will be shared by the five brothers whose duty it will be to carry on the firm. Stephen adores his mother, respects his father, and has an unquestioning commitment to his family. And the family, it seems, has an unquestioning commitment to the stability of the family firm. Stephen's solidarity with his brothers, his loyalty to the family code, is unquestioning. His passion and his commitment to Ethel is lifelong; but within his family he cannot stand up for her. He doesn't want to cross them.

A Letter to Stephen, 1916

Among Eliza's papers, Eva finds a letter addressed to Stephen at the front, dated August 1916. It is written on elegant business letterhead carrying a smart line drawing of the Feher furniture store, which is close to the recently built Basilica in the centre of town—a prestigious location. The letter is written by the paterfamilias, Sigmund:

Dear Son, Stephen!
We were pleased to hear from your letter that you are well. Of course, it is a matter of pride for us that all the five of you are doing your duty for our country, but we are also understandably worried about you all, eager to hear from you. I know you will take your responsibility to write seriously.

I also want to draw your attention to the bank account I opened for the family in A., in Austria. Should you or your brothers need money in foreign currency while you are abroad, you should have this account accessible to each of you. I want you, Son, to realize this, and take advantage of it whenever you may need it. I know you well enough to be sure you would not abuse this privilege.

Your dear Mother and I are getting along quite well. Last Sunday we visited our two grandchildren, Heidi and Agnes, in Svabhegy, where the family is renting a villa for the summer; the mountain air agrees with the little girls. They are well, rosy cheeked, healthy, and developing mentally and physically. While Andrew and Frank are on the front, I feel it is my duty as the head of the family to make sure their wives and children are well looked after and feel the hardships of these wartime years as little as possible. Business is doing well. Both your Mother and I think of you all and keep you in our prayers. Waiting for your next letter,

Your loving father,
Sigmund

FEHÉR ZSIGMOND FURNITURE
LÁZÁR-UTCA 3
(In the vicinity of the Bazilika)

Letter to Stephen from his father, Sigmund, 1916

At the time, Heidi and Agnes are two-year-old toddlers, the same age as Eliza. Yet there is not one word about Stephen's little daughter or about Sigmund's sense of duty to look after the welfare of Stephen's spouse and child.

The last page of Stephen's small diary catalogues and summarizes all the letters and cards from and to Ethel: "Wrote to Ethel on Sunday. Why doesn't she take the little one to the doctor?" "Wrote to Ethel Wednesday. What did doctor say?" "Wrote to Ethel again. Why does she not write more frequently?"

Photograph of Baby Eliza, 1916

Baby Eliza is given out to a woman in the country who runs a "baby farm," looking after babies whose parents are in no position to supervise them closely. These are Eliza's first childhood memories.

I must be very small. There are several beds in the dark room. In the middle of the night I wake up to the urge to urinate, but I don't want to get out of the warm bed, leave the warm house for the cold, the dark. The dark outside is worse than the dark inside. The outhouse seems so far away and I dread crossing the courtyard. I wet the bed. At first it is warm, then it turns cold. I'm smothered by guilt and fear. The woman with the red face will beat me when she sees what I did. I crawl to a relatively dry corner of the bed, hugging myself, whimpering. I don't dare to cry, to wake her and get a beating. Her idea of toilet training is to tie the child to the potty. I'm tied down until I finish my business. Later when I still make a mistake and dirty myself, the woman with the red face makes me taste my excrement.

I also remember that there are special preparations when visitors are expected. I'm spruced up, given a special treat, told to be very good … It probably means not to complain. But how could I complain? I fear these two strangers who come to visit me, whom I should call Mother and Father, almost as much as I fear the woman with the red face looking after me. For a long time I simply don't know what it means to complain. But I must be a sickly, unhappy-looking infant, because "Aunt Mother"

Three-year-old Eliza and her visitor, "Aunt Mother"

sometimes takes me with her to town, to the doctor's office, and then I also have to take the foul-tasting medication.

Later on Eva finds photographs of Agnes and Heidi, but there are definitely no pictures of Sigmund among Eliza's papers.

Eliza's Photograph, 1925

The next photo shows Eliza as a girl of eleven or twelve. She is wearing a big bow in her short, cropped hair, just long enough to cover her big ears, which she is so self-conscious about. It was taken in a studio: like many posed photographs from that era, her expression is serious, dramatic. Her deep brown eyes are wide open and inquiring.

There is a story attached to this picture. The story of the three slaps. Eva can still hear her mother tell it, her deep voice so rich in feeling, so full of irony.

"Have I ever told you the story of the three slaps?" Eliza would always begin. "By this time I was being invited to my father's family, first every once in a while, then quite regularly. In his own way he was letting his family know that I did belong to him, that in my own way I also had to be accepted.

"You must remember the house in O Street, where I took you in 1945 after the ghetto was liberated. In the twenties every Feher had an apartment in that house, except for my father, who shared an apartment with his youngest brother, Willie, and Willie's beautiful and sophisticated wife, Renée.

"Renée wafts around in a cocoon of silk, jewellery, and perfume, and has her hand kissed not only by the children in the family, but also by her admirers who visit her. All of my father's sisters-in-law have admirers. With their glamorous fur boas thrown over their shoulders, they smile at me vacantly from under their elaborate hats. Their beauty is set off by fur, feathers, tasteful jewellery, and clouds of fine perfume as they climb in and out of taxis on their way to their elegant parties.

"I enter their vast apartments with their crystal chandeliers, marble statuary. I walk across shiny parquet floors muffled with thick Persian carpets. I arrive at these visits open, innocent, vulnerable, pleased to be invited to play with Heidi and Agnes, my pretty, well-dressed, well-bred cousins. Often we're joined by Bandi, who is a few years older than we are. He is Renée's son from her first marriage. I entertain them all by improvising games, or writing plays that we all act together.

"When I cannot come, the girls run up to my father, lacing their arms in his: 'Stephen, Uncle Stephen, Why didn't you bring along Eliza to play with us?'

"I'm twelve at the time.

"One day we decide to go to the municipal swimming pool on the island, all of us, Heidi, Agnes, Bandi, and I. Bandi is between fourteen and fifteen, a spoiled, handsome, mischievous young boy. While we're playing in the pool, he pushes me down and holds me under the water so long I almost drown. When finally he lets go of me, I'm gasping for air. I cry when I get home, and tell Mother about it. Later she tells Father.

"Father becomes very quiet when he hears what happened. He turns around, marches home to the apartment he shares with Willie's family, and without a word of explanation slaps Bandi's face, hard.

"The next week I arrive at their apartment in my blue velvet jumper and with a big bow in my hair—Mother always makes sure I wear my Sunday best for these visits. The maid answers the door, but Aunt Renée is already standing there to greet me.

"'I kiss the hand, Aunt Renée,' I curtsy, while she hovers over me, her tall, statuesque presence a hazy apparition of silk, jewellery, and clouds of perfume.

"'You little tattletale,' she says. 'You sly little thing. Acting like butter wouldn't melt in your mouth, and then telling tales about my son behind my back.'

"Her pale, impressive face viciously distorted, her beautiful auburn bangs all out of place, suddenly she raises her impeccably manicured hand and without warning slaps my face hard.

"I run downstairs crying, across the road and straight into Father's wood-panelled office on the main floor of the furniture store.

"'Father, Father, I got a big slap from Aunt Renée.' The mark of her fingers must still be on my face. Father rises from his desk. He's turned white and very silent. He says nothing, he just stands up, walks over to the apartment house with a heavy stride, marches upstairs, opens the door with his key, walks up to this sophisticated socialite dressed in the latest Parisian fashion, the way she always is, and gives her an enormous slap on the face.

"Then, still without a word, he takes me by the hand and turns toward the door.

Twelve-year-old Eliza and the story of the Three Slaps

"Renée starts to scream. Her husband, Willie, comes out of his study in his impeccably tailored silk smoking jacket.

"'Renée! My God, what's happened? What's happened? For God's sake will someone tell me what's happened?'

"When he hears his beloved wife's accusations against his older brother, he breaks down and starts to cry like a little boy. This, of course, doesn't endear him or his brother-in-law to Renée. At any rate, a big family feud breaks out. I don't speak to the Fehers for years or set foot in any of their apartments. But I don't mind—Father has stood up for me. There can be no doubt in my heart anymore that he's my father. Yet is he or is he not my mother's husband?

"It's that same year, in school, that I first hear the word 'illegitimate.' The girls mention it in a whisper, with what sounds like a sneer. And of course, I've already noticed that Mother never comes with me to the Fehers, although there's no question she knows them quite well. And why is it that all the other women—the mothers of Agi, Heidi, and Bandi— are living in the same elegant apartment house, each with her husband? And why does Mother have to live somewhere else with me? Even if Father stays with us much of the time, why does he have a place with them also? You see, for years I have no answer to these questions."

Photograph of Ethel and Eliza Wearing Hats, 1931

The next picture shows Ethel and Eliza, each wearing a smart travelling hat with a little veil around the brim. In her late thirties, Ethel is tense, her expression grim and determined. Eliza is seventeen. Her deep-brown eyes have known sadness, but they're also full of expectation. The picture has been taken at the train station. Ethel is taking her daughter to Paris. Eliza is going to stay there for a year, in a well-known language school close to Les Invalides and the Rodin Museum. What the seventeen-year-old Eliza does not realize is that at the time, Ethel is fighting a decisive battle for her daughter's future. She has finally presented Stephen with an ultimatum.

The two of them agree that a girl has no alternative but marriage. Ethel insists that their daughter's chance for marriage—her entire future—is at stake. And Eliza will have

Ethel and Eliza in travelling hats

to face the question soon. Ethel has waited long enough. Unless Stephen can make up his mind to marry her over his family's opposition, Ethel will emigrate with his daughter, either to Brazil to join her sister Helen or to France to join her brother Auri. Ethel is ready to start a new life, to live without the stigma of Eliza's illegitimacy. It is Ethel who suggests to Stephen that they send Eliza away for a year while the two of them come to a decision.

A Letter to Eliza, 1931

Next, Eva pulls from the big brown envelope a letter Ethel wrote to Eliza. It is clear that Ethel is struggling on two fronts: she wants to ensure her daughter's future and at the same time to win her love and trust:

My dear daughter Eliza:
Thank you for your delightful letter from Paris. If you only knew how I miss you when I read your amusing, funny letters. If only we could get along as well also when you come home. My dear daughter, enjoy yourself, but also take care of your health, and, among other things, watch your weight. Resist all that delicious Swiss chocolate they serve you after each meal ...

Eva hasn't seen this letter before. Yet in it she can hear Eliza's voice, telling her side of the story:

"Imagine suddenly finding yourself in the capital of the world. And the contrast between my mother's one-room apartment and this most elegant boarding school in the middle of Paris, right next to the Rodin Museum, to Les Invalides ... On the weekends most of the boarders go out on passes. But my parents don't give their permission that I go out by myself or with friends. In vain do I send my letters begging Mother for a pass.

"Mother, why don't you trust me? All the other girls are going to relatives, to friends, or they simply go out together. Only I remain in the Lycée, all alone, looking out the window like a prisoner.

"Of course I eat all the chocolate I can lay my hands on. We're offered baskets of chocolate after every meal—by the end of the first five months I've put on thirty pounds ...

"But I'm still like a prisoner starving in the midst of plenty—a prisoner in the most exciting city in the world. The glamour of the streets, the shops, the lights, the theatres, the music right outside my window ...

"But my mother doesn't listen to me.

"The only people who take me out occasionally are Uncle Auri and his wife. He is Mother's eldest brother who emigrated to Paris in the mid-twenties. He is a watchmaker and his wife, Jolie, a piano teacher, but both of them are happy they found jobs as workers in the Renault factory. With their little girl, Edie, they live in the suburbs in a one-room apartment without a bathroom. Whenever they can, they come for me to the Lycée and take me to their home for the weekend. Auri and Jolie give up their own bed—they simply would not hear of their guest sleeping on the floor. On Sunday the four of us go on long walks in the Luxembourg Gardens."

This is the most exciting year in Eliza's young life. She has the opportunity to learn a new language, and in a few months she speaks it like a native. (Years later she will learn Russian in less than a year, well enough to work as a translator). Eliza enjoys the school, her classmates from all over the world, and her teachers. Her art teacher recommends that she try for admission at the Fine Arts Academy.

There is no doubt that Eliza's parents are proud of her achievements, but they will not hear about higher education for her. What purpose would it serve? A girl has to get married; no profession is an alternative for marriage. And art school, of course, is completely out of the question. It is not practical, and what's more, it is not respectable. There are nudes in the life drawing classes. Stephen and Ethel associate art school with the loose life of bohemians—surely not a respectable environment for a well-brought-up young girl. And both parents find it extremely important not only that Eliza be well brought up, but also that she be seen that way. Eva can still hear the bitterness in Eliza's voice, her lifetime's worth of disappointment and resentment:

"You see, Eva, all this would have been different if I were a boy. They didn't trust me because I was a girl. If only I could have gotten what I wanted then, when I still had the opportunity. 'No daughter of mine,' I swore then to myself, 'no daughter of mine will ever be allowed to go through this, to end up totally dependent on marriage, on a husband.' I promised myself then that come what may, my daughters would have their independence, their own profession."

Reading Ethel's letter today, Eva also recognizes her grandmother's struggle. She is working hard to establish the terms for Eliza's respectable middle-class future, but that is not what she writes to her daughter about. As her letter makes clear, she wants to be friends with Eliza: she is so pleased to have detailed letters about Paris. And she also wants to share with her some of her own life, her own hopes and anxieties. Ignatius, Ethel's father, is growing old and feeble. Stephen has always been generous and kind to the old man. Ethel has also been busy with the details of their new house. Would Eliza embroider another of those colourful cushions everyone admires so much, for the living room sofa?

Eliza with Diamond Earrings, 1932

Not long after Ethel's letter about the Swiss chocolate, Stephen and Ethel have a quiet civil wedding and begin to make a home together like any respectable middle-class couple. When Eliza returns from Paris, she finds that her home is now an elegant villa in the suburbs, a healthy hour-long walk for Stephen to the store every day. Most of the time, Eliza walks with him. Ethel is now one of the rich Mrs. Fehers, like the mothers of Agi, Heidi, and Bandi. Her picture from this time shows a serenely smiling woman wearing glittering diamond earrings that complement the light in her warm brown eyes.

So, suddenly, Eliza has a new address, a new name, and a new religion (she has converted back from Catholicism, the religion in which she was raised.) She is now unquestionably her father's daughter. And this, of course, also means she has become an heiress, a highly eligible, intelligent, and attractive young girl back from finishing school in Paris—she has become a commodity on the marriage market.

There is a photograph of Eliza in a ball gown. There are also several pictures of Eliza with her cousin Agi, both of them shown entertaining eligible young men at the villa. The photos are landmarks of Ethel's success: she has finally won the battle she fought so long for her daughter. Eliza lives the life of the well-to-do; closely chaperoned by Ethel, she goes to dances, to parties; she is very much sought after.

"We had some wonderful parties with Agi during this time," Eliza used to tell her daughter. "Once we were at a dance in Buda, and Agi and I had several young men in our tow. After the dance, it was a mild summer night, the young men suggested they walk us home, at least part of the way. While we crossed the Franz Josef Bridge, arm in arm with Agnes and Mother, they followed a few steps behind us, giving us the most beautiful serenade. Emery was a young man, one of my beaux I really liked. He had an especially powerful tenor voice, and it carried beautifully over the Danube. Unfortunately, my parents decided he was not to be taken seriously. Ethel and Stephen enjoyed his company, but they suspected him of being a bohemian."

Ethel with diamond earrings at the villa, 1932

Underneath the photographs marking Ethel's success as a mother of a debutante, Eva finds a small envelope with a yellowed clipping from the classified pages of one of the capital's major dailies:

ELIZA COME HOME. URGENT. MOTHER SERIOUSLY ILL

After Eliza comes home from Paris to her new life, her parents follow her success with joy, but also with anxiety. Ethel probably never feels quite at ease with the light, frivolous banter that is so fashionable among the young people of the upper-middle class in the early thirties. And Stephen has always been suspicious of the late hours, the daring modern dances. He and Ethel paid a steep price in their youth for losing respectability, and now they guard their daughter with a strange mixture of pride and puritanical fear.

"I felt they simply did not trust me," Eliza once explained. There were totally unfounded reproaches, recriminations, suspicions. There were long, angry arguments. After an especially humiliating scene with her parents, Eliza ran away. She took a train to a small town and spent two days in the local hotel. On the third day she opened the newspaper to find her parents' message. She took the first train home.

Eliza's Engagement Picture, 1933

There followed a period of deep concern on both sides, followed by various attempts at reconciliation. But genuine peace did not come until Eliza, right after her nineteenth birthday, fell in love and got engaged to a handsome, ambitious young engineer, Leslie. The wedding date was set for November 1933. For the young couple's honeymoon, Stephen and Ethel made them a gift especially valuable during that time of strict currency regulations: a six-week trip to Rome, Venice, the Riviera, Paris …

In 1983, the year after Eliza's death, Eva goes to Paris for a short vacation with her husband and Judy. She takes herself around Paris, trying to see it the way Eliza might have in the early 1930s. Les Invalides, the Rodin Museum, the bridges along the Seine must have been the same. Eva and Judy even go to Eliza's boarding school, but find it locked up and abandoned. But the reunion with Edie, Uncle Auri's daughter, is unexpectedly warm. Cousin Edie invites them to dinner in her small, comfortable apartment, and afterwards takes out the family album.

"Look, Eva, I have something to show you. And if you don't have it already, I would like you to take it."

It is a picture of Stephen and Ethel's villa, a two-storey stuccoed house with a mansard roof and a large balcony with white stone balustrades. Taken from the street, the picture does not show the garden, only a single rosebush peeking over the fence. A little girl and a middle-aged couple are standing on the balcony.

"I spent some weeks at your grandparents' house when I was a little girl, on a visit to Budapest," Edie tells them. "They had just moved into their new villa. They were wonderful people, so very happy with the beautiful house and garden. Ethel was an excellent housewife, and their home was full of beautifully kept houseplants. Also, she was generosity itself; she arranged for Lenke, her cook and housekeeper, to live in the service apartment with her illegitimate little daughter and treated both with great kindness. Eliza herself was a marvellous cook and a warm, generous hostess. But also—how shall I put it?—it mattered to her very much how the maid served the main course, even when it was only her own brother's family at the table. She was very conventional, a typical bourgeois.

"But Stephen, your grandfather, he was truly an interesting man. He would sit down with me and pick up a metal pea can that got emptied and discarded. In a matter of minutes he would transform it into a little stove for my dolls, complete with a door for logs—the logs were made of matchsticks—and even a chimney. He was simply marvellous with children. And no difficulties about class, age, language. *Un homme extraordinaire, vraiment extraordinaire.*"

Eva is not really surprised. It is simply one more irony that Ethel, the poor girl who had spent her life ostracized and humiliated by narrow bourgeois thinking, turned into a bourgeois with a vengeance. Trying to live up to her new position, she was anxious to show herself to be as good at this game as her well-bred, sophisticated sisters-in-law—who still did not accept her, of course.

Eva encounters an interesting dilemma when she comes to her next two finds:

The photograph of the engagement reception was taken in the heavily decorated living and dining rooms of the villa. There is the new family: the groom's parents, Joseph and Betty, the groom's brothers and sisters, and Leslie, the groom himself. And there is the entire Feher family: Stephen with his brothers and their wives, including Renée with her auburn bangs and long cigarette holder. And between a solemn Stephen and a somewhat bewildered Eliza, there is Ethel, beaming. But what about Ethel's family? Where are the poor relatives? Where are the Bergers? Ethel's mother has passed away, but where is Ignatius,

Eliza and Leslie's engagement party, Budapest, 1933

Ethel's father? Is he ill, or has he not been invited for fear he might not "fit in" with the rest?

And who would have made that decision? In her letter from Brazil, Aunt Helen, Ethel's youngest sister, asks the same question. Her letters reflect the deeply felt sentimentality of the lower-middle-class women of her age. She congratulates Eliza and Ethel effusively. Then she puts her question:

"Our family is scattered. If you only knew how I miss you, how I long now to be among you in Budapest. But my dear Ethel and Eliza, I must ask, although I fear to ask: 'Why is it I don't see my father in the picture?'"

Eliza does not have the answer, or perhaps she simply doesn't want to share it. And now Eva can never have the answer.

Pictures from the Villa and Pages from Stephen's Diary, 1941

There follow now pictures of Sandy and Eva as infants in the front rose garden of Stephen and Ethel's villa. Eva's earliest memories include some magical moments in that garden. She is looking for the Easter Bunny's gifts (hidden in the grass by Grandma Ethel); in the vegetable garden she is looking for the tiny carrots and turnips that Ethel allows her to take

In the villa, Stephen with Sandy and Eliza, in joy and in mourning

In the villa, Eliza, Ethel, Sandy, and Eva

home for her dollies; she is flying into the arms of her grandmother, who has crouched to welcome her. Stephen and Ethel beam with pride and joy as they hold Sandy and Eva in their arms.

Eva pastes the next item into the album with great care. Two yellowing pages have been torn from a diary. Once again, it is Stephen's handwriting. They seem to be letters to his wife, but on closer reading it becomes clear that they are actually prayers, meditations addressed to her after her premature death from a stroke. She was forty-six.

So 1941 is a year of mourning. Stephen's words are those of a broken man haunted by guilt, regret, and a sense of loss from which he will never free himself. Though devoted to each other for nearly thirty years, he and Ethel lived together, happily, for less then ten. He is determined to devote the rest of his life to his daughter and his two granddaughters, Sandy and Eva. But a few years later, he too will be dead—murdered by the Nazis.

The maze of faces, of lives. Is there any way out?

A way to the centre? In the letters and photographs in her new–old album, Eva recognizes a curious pattern. Together they are like a set of dominos. The dots of guilt … Dots matched by dots by dots … Guilt begetting guilt begetting guilt …

Yet the line of guilt is not quite unbroken. On the other side of each domino are dots of love. You can place these dots next to each other as well. Love begetting love? Love begetting guilt?

Where does guilt end; where does love begin?
Eva wants to assemble her mother's portrait.
But now the big brown envelope is almost empty.
The last two pieces of writing are both from the summer of 1944.

A Note to Eliza, 1944

The first item is a torn, irregular piece of paper, thin, almost transparent, with a note in pale ink. Stephen has written it from the internment camp in the Hungarian town of Kistarcsa, where he has been taken with other prosperous Jews now that the Germans have marched into Hungary.

"My dearest Eliza: The Germans have just dragged out a hundred men from among our midst. Nobody knows why. They are going to be shot. Dear daughter Eliza: take the children; you must go into hiding right away."

Unlike those stamped, green-edged postcards Stephen has been allowed to send home sometimes, each of them initialled by the censor, this note is torn around the edges. It must have been smuggled out, perhaps furled around a pencil, because forty years later, the irregular creases are still there.

A Postcard from Eliza, 1944

The last item is one of the official postcards with the censor's stamp: Received July 1944. It is a card Eliza has written to Leslie, who is serving in a labour battalion. Leslie must have carried this card with him for the next eight months, because he brought it home with him in February 1945:

"My Dearest: Stop worrying about us and trying to give us advice from the distance. I know what we are allowed, what we are able to do—you can have no idea, being so far from us. My dearest, please, take good care of yourself and stop worrying about us. The children are well: they still know no fear."

Eva is shocked. She wishes she could turn to her mother:

"No doubt you think you were right. And of course you worked so hard to protect us from fear. But my fear, the fear that envelopes the world of the six-year-old like a dark vapour ... How could you have missed it?

"Is it possible you did not see my fear?

"Yet you're right in a way.

"The fear I feel is not really fear for my life. It is clear to me that should a bomb strike close to me, should anyone try to hit, maim, or murder me, your body stands between me and the pain, between me and death. At the bottom of the vortex of fear there is a centre of absolute calm. It is you, Mother, who is at the centre. In my heart at the age of six, there is absolute certainty that as long as you are there, you will dig me out of the rubble, you will shield me from the explosion, you will protect me from the blows of evil men. I fear all of that, yet that is not really what I fear.

"No, the fear is not for my own life directly. But outside this calm centre there is a fear nevertheless, and it is reaching out for me, trying to grab me whenever I close my eyes, whenever I'm not careful. It is the fear for *you*, my support, my flesh-and-blood shelter. The close shelter of your lap, your arms around me. If I were to lose you, I would be lost without hope, without sight, without the power or will to go on!"

There are no more photographs to paste into the album—no pictures had been taken during the war years. Yet Eva feels she cannot allow the continuity to be broken. Almost without noticing it, she has pulled out her notebook and started writing her answer to her mother. She cannot give up now on the family album, even though the pictures that should follow here are pictures fixed only in her memory. To retrieve those pictures, she will have to go deeper and deeper into that tunnel: the tunnel of the family past has taken her into a tunnel even darker and narrower, to her own childhood, the very centre of her being, the very centre of her ties with her mother.

THE TUNNEL
1944–1945

1.

The convent.

The early-morning expeditions to the bathroom.

In November it is still pitch dark at six in the morning, and the old-fashioned bathroom with its huge yellow tub and unheated geyser is at the end of an unlit corridor. It is dark and cold when Mother wakes me. Sleepy and apprehensive, I am also somewhat excited by the adventure: to think that I'll again undress and get washed in cold water in that dark cold place. I stagger behind Mother. She carries our towel, the soap and our clothes, always in a hurry, feeling her way along the corridor walls in the dusk. If we want to have enough time, we have to be there before the others. Getting up so early in the dark gives us an edge over them; we don't have to wait and endure the impatient or snide remarks of the other mothers and children while they wait their turn.

On these expeditions Mother, Sandy, and I become one body, one soul; we shall stand united against the outside world, the shortages, the filth, the cold, the lack of privacy. And by concentrating on the details of our day-to-day existence within the walls of the convent, we also somehow push the real threat farther and farther away. Because we are here to hide from that threat. Even I, at the age of six, know that we should never criticize, argue, or disagree with the silent, distant-looking nuns floating along the corridors in their white habits.

The nuns are hiding us, the thirty-odd women and children who sleep together in the dormitory. They're also feeding us, at the long wooden tables in the refectory. In fact I am quite willing to be grateful and loving: I like the simple elegance of their cool, starched white habits, the hushed tone of their conversations, the superior calm of their silence. I also love to go to chapel with its glowing candles and the smell of incense. I am awed by the mild, gentle Christ on the crucifix and by the wonderfully translucent beads of the rosaries the nuns have distributed among us children before service. I am delighted to have my very own rosary, although at first it is quite a dilemma whether to reach for the shiny black one or the rose-coloured transparent one that reminds me of a chime. I decide on the latter. I love fingering the angular beads and listening to the melodious chanting of the Lord's Prayer: "Our Father who art in Heaven ..."

But the one that really touches me is the Hail Mary. The word for "grace" in Hungarian is *malaszt,* and I don't quite know why, but this archaic word, which nobody uses anymore, conjures up for me a landscape in diffused light after rain. The fresh fragrance of rain over summer grass. A landscape in which I can be consoled, calmed, soothed after tears. This word, which I don't understand at all, is also, to me, a colour. *Malaszt* is the colour of the transparent celluloid rattle, my only memento from my infancy and a gift from my dead grandmother, something I had to leave behind in my nursery just recently. And when it comes to the "fruit of thy womb, Jesus," it seems to me there is a deep silence and then a rising, lilting, fascinating melody. The ripening of fruit. The fullness of time. A lovely, graceful vessel brimming over slowly, very slowly, with cool, fresh water. (In Hungarian the word for womb is also the word for bee, so in my mind the ripening of the fruit of the womb is becoming indistinguishable from the ripening of the fruit after the sweet labours of the bee. The words bring back the fragrance of golden-green pears on a silent summer morning in a mountain orchard like the one I visited with my grandfather only the past summer.)

At the same time, I have a vague notion that the fruit of the bee and the baby Jesus may somehow mean the same thing after all. I love babies, and even in the midst of my confusion I am drawn to some kind of a deep joy behind the veiled magic of the word. A word with its own colour and fragrance, opening up memories of my own recent childhood before the German occupation. March, half a year ago. At the age of six, I recall with nostalgia these memories of when I was closer to five. It is an era that has already faded into the past and been lost irretrievably.

When the nuns make us children draw pictures at the long refectory tables, I use my whole share of coloured pencils to draw cemeteries with long, long rows of crosses, each drawing invariably backlit by a glowing red sunset. Deep down I am convinced that my multitude of glowing crosses must be the most beautiful thing the nuns have ever seen—I am drowning in the melancholy of the cross, the beads of the rosary, the light through the stained glass windows on the thick, whitewashed walls of our little chapel.

Yet in spite of all this, there is a holding back: I am conscious of some kind of reticence in Mother, in my sister, and in the nuns themselves. There are probably several reasons for it. To begin with, though I'm often moved to tears by the nuns' silent kindness in offering me rosaries and coloured pencils, one day to my shock I overhear that we have all had to pay for being given this shelter. Father, God knows how, must have paid once he learned of this hiding place next to the barracks of his labour battalion. Occasionally I still wonder whether he paid enough and whether all the coloured pencils were included. If for some reason the money is not enough, how long will we be allowed to stay? Will the nuns turn us over to the Germans if we run out of money?

And there is something else, another kind of payment, perhaps even more important. Because unlike many other mothers and children with whom we share the dormitory, the three of us are not going to convert. Of course the question has come up. It is Sandy who with her customary decisive manner declares that we should not abandon our religion under any circumstances. Mother says that this resolution would certainly please our forefathers in heaven. I don't quite understand why we should be so concerned about pleasing our forefathers at this moment (or who they are exactly), but on the whole I feel proud to be part of Mother's and Sandy's resolution.

Yet I can't avoid noticing that it would obviously please the nuns to convert us. They do not apply pressure directly, but they don't need to. The protection of the Pope's letter—something one can still buy if one knows where and has the money—must be based on the Pope's expectation that we Jews know the rules of polite behaviour. By offering us protection, the Pope is showing us the gentle, generous kindness of Christ, so wouldn't it only be appropriate for us to express our appreciation by converting to Christianity?

Many of the mothers around us seem to be reasoning my way. "Why should I not do it, if it might help me and my children?" argues Mrs. Jonalsky, a frail but tenacious schoolteacher with two daughters our age. Mrs. Jonalsky is smart and tough and would do anything to ensure their survival. She can also be catty and malicious. She laughs out loud when the other children make fun of Sandy, calling her Miss Fatso. And I agree with Mother that although she is a schoolteacher, she doesn't really show much kindness to or understanding of children. I guess it is mainly to avoid Mrs. Jonalsky and her sharp tongue that Mother wakes us up so early for the bathroom.

Even so, Mrs. Jonalsky makes cutting remarks about our going there before her. She insinuates that we have aristocratic airs, insisting as we do on taking a shower or having a thorough rub-down every single day.

"As if it will really matter how clean you are when they come to take us," she says with a disdainful laugh, mainly for the benefit of the other occupants of the dormitory.

Mother must know that in a way, Mrs. Jonalsky is right. The Germans or the Hungarian Arrow Cross could burst into our lives at any moment. They could drag us into the ghetto, and even the children have heard the rumour that the ghetto has been mined so that the Germans can blow it up whenever they choose.

And there are, of course, other rumours we overhear from the grown-ups. The river. Forced marches to the border. Deportations. What exactly these words mean I try not to think about. I am preoccupied, nevertheless, with one particular detail of these facelessly looming horrors that I overheard several months ago. "The children," whispered one of the adults in that hushed tone I now identify with news I ought not to hear, "the children will be the first. They're snipped off, separated from the parents right at the beginning." I don't know what lies in store for us and I refuse to picture it. But the notion of being "snipped off" has come to signify a fear that fills my private world like a dark vapour.

2.

To be snipped off. By last spring, when the Germans marched into Hungary, our family had spent most of a year in the Matra Mountains to escape the bombing of the capital. Father and Grandfather stayed in the city during the week to mind the store but joined us on weekends. For us children the year was an extended holiday, although Sandy did attend the village school so as not to lose all of grade two. We went on long excursions, skiing in the winter, hiking in the spring.

Then as soon as the Germans came in, in March, they brought a decree that Jews were permitted to stay only in the big centres. Since we were residents of Budapest, we were supposed to go back there, except that the bombing was still the worst in the capital. There were also rumours about families being taken off the train, the children being separated and sent to mysterious destinations. So our parents decided to keep away from Budapest and move down to Gyongyos, the town closest to the Matra Mountains.

In Gyongyos we rented a cottage for the spring and awaited new developments. The yellow star was introduced, and we all had to wear it on the street. I remember Tante, our elegant blond governess, coming to visit us in Gyongyos. With a laugh she pointed to her stylish leather handbag, then pulled out the yellow star she had been keeping in it. She had been living with us for three years and I had become deeply attached to her, yet now, suddenly, I saw her as a distant, mysterious stranger. Imagine the risk she had taken in not wearing the star. Or was it more likely she was lying to us now about being Jewish? How could one refuse to wear the yellow star so casually!

The white-haired lady in her sixties from whom we rent the house welcomes us with bread and salt when we move in. I find this a strange but touching gesture of hospitality. Mother, though, is not touched very deeply. The rent for people who wear the yellow star is astronomically high.

Quite a few middle-class Jewish families from Budapest are staying in Gyongyos for the same reasons we are. This is the first time Mother is without domestic help, and Sandy and I busy ourselves with chores. But we still have time to meet casually with the other Budapest families, mainly mothers and children, all of us brought together by the yellow star.

It is May, and somehow the days are filled with the smell of lilacs and the mellifluous tune of a popular song:

The month of May, the month of May,
The month of blooooooming peonies.

It wafts from the street whenever someone opens a window, whenever we turn on the radio:

The pangs of love, sweet pangs of love.
I fell for the spell of your maaa-gic.

It seems that everyone is singing or humming the same song to celebrate May, the sweet promise of summers to come. The song goes on and on about spells, pangs, and intoxication, until my head is reeling. Listening to the song, I somehow grow more aware of the boys my age around me. When is the magic supposed to start? Am I expected to know? Will they somehow know?

Ivan Gardos is one of my friends in Gyongyos. His parents own a small bookstore in Budapest. He's a year older and thinks himself far more wise to the world. I remember us sauntering ahead of our mothers along a country lane on the outskirts of town. The grass is green, the sun is shining, each of us is licking an ice cream, and I'm wondering what people mean by "pangs of love." (The meaning of "irresistible" I have already checked with Mother.) Ivan and I are enjoying our ice cream; it is chocolate and vanilla.

Then Ivan, no doubt to impress me, does something reckless. With a sweep of his arm he throws his empty ice cream cone far away into the green field that borders the road.

"Throwing away good food!" his mother scolds him. "Aren't you ashamed of yourself? Let's hope you won't have reason to regret it." Those simple words keep echoing in my head because of their ominous intimations of our future. I'm not at all surprised to hear that one does not throw away food easily. After all, there's a war on. I've also read a fairy tale about the girl who was punished for life because she stepped on a piece of bread. That was bad enough. But should an ice cream cone be taken as seriously as a piece of bread? After all, Ivan did not step on it. It would be good to understand what exactly he did wrong. And what could be the punishment? Because there is the threat of some kind of punishment. Will Ivan really regret throwing away the ice cream cone so carelessly? And why? For his part, Ivan isn't at all bothered. He listens to the warning with total incomprehension and a smart-alecky expression on his mischievous, freckled face.

Then, from one day to the next, we're told that all the Jews in Gyongyos must move into the ghetto. We have to pack and leave the sunny, comfortable cottage. Each of us can take only a limited weight in packages. Most of our things, including my favourite dolls, are carted away for safekeeping. ("Mr. Nagy or Mr. Kovacs says he will save it for us," is how my parents and our friends refer to this, and in all fairness they probably should have added, "At least he says so now." Later I hear my parents comment wryly: "Let's hope he won't be keeping it safely to himself.")

We can still return to Budapest, but my parents' fear of the train journey must be strong, because they agree we should rather move into the Gyongyos ghetto. Only after we find ourselves in the fenced-in area between rows of rough shacks surrounded by deep mud softened by the recent rain, does the picture present itself in an entirely new light. The grounds have recently been vacated by cholera patients.

"What is cholera, Mummy?"

"Hush, I'll explain another time."

Isolated from the rest of the town, the whole ghetto smells of neglect, dirt, and disinfectants. To get to the outhouse, one has to wade through mud. And in the outhouse, foul-smelling mud has risen to the brim of the seats.

We're surrounded by our luggage. Although we have had to observe the restrictions in terms of weight, we have elegant, sturdy leather cases, and parcels wrapped in heavy woollen blankets. Mother looks around and cannot bring herself to unpack.

To see Mother cry.

All through these months she has been unshakable in her faith: we're going to make it, no matter what. Suddenly she breaks down in sobs. Father watches her shoulders quiver, then turns on his heel. He has changed his mind instantly. It is the very last day he can act, just a few hours before the gates slam shut, a few hours before—something no one expects—the ghetto is to be surrounded with barbed wire.

Father rushes out of the ghetto, through the streets to the police station. We need a permit to leave the Gyongyos ghetto and return to our residence in Budapest. In an hour he is back with our papers. He has returned in a horse-driven carriage, with a mustachioed coachman. The two men quickly load our unopened baggage.

I am reassured to watch them load the heavy, colourful horsehair blanket with its white, yellow, and red stripes. The blanket had belonged to Grandfather during the Great War. Today, rolled up, it contains those very few toys Mother has insisted on saving. As we later find out, Father has arranged for the safekeeping of all these with a local policeman.

And now we are free to rush ahead with only a few pieces of hand luggage to catch the Budapest train. Had Mother not started to cry, she, who had been so anxious to put on a brave face, to spare us fear, and had Father not been so decisive to get us out before they shut the gate, there would be no one here now to remember. Not one of the women or children with whom we spent that spring in Gyongyos has returned from the concentration camps.

The month of May, the month of love,
The month of blooooooming peonies ...

The song will remain a hit for years and years, surviving the war, surviving the change of regimes after the war. I can never listen to its cheap, deceptive sensuality without a catch in my throat. It always brings back my friend Ivan with the ice cream cone, and the total incomprehension on his freckled, mischievous face.

At that moment, of course, all I know is that we have to face that long-postponed train journey. I am keenly aware of the threat: "Children may be snipped off." The words I have overheard echo in my mind endlessly. The train is crowded; people slouch in the corridors, lean against the walls, or sit on their suitcases. I stay very quiet, keeping close to Mother, Father, and Sandy for the three or four hours it takes. Then the train pulls into Keleti Station. I remember the excitement of the bitter smoky smell permeating the huge glass-covered iron hall, the sudden rush of porters and passengers, the tremendous sense of relief that we're back in this big city full of life, the joyous anticipation of seeing our home, our neighbours, the toys in our nursery, which I have not seen for almost a year.

3.

And then it happens.

Leaving the compartment in the tow of my family I am getting ready to climb off the train. I'm on the crowded metal steps—how steep and frightening they seem—when suddenly I feel a short, painful tug at my hair. I'm wearing braids, but my hair is soft and unruly, and a lock on the front must have gotten loose, because some vicious and hostile force is pulling it from somewhere far above me. Getting down the stairs, I'm pulled along this way for several steps.

Wincing, with tears in my eyes, I become blind and benumbed to my surroundings. Engulfed by a sense of looming disaster, I finally recognize the horrible, larger-than-life significance of that dreaded word. There's no hope of fending it off; I've been singled out, captured, and now I'm being dragged away. I've been snipped from my mother.

It takes time for me to return to my senses, to see once more the world swirling around me.

"I'm sorry, little girl," I hear as I slowly come to.

It's the voice of a passenger whose button got caught in my hair. As quickly as he can in the midst of the pulsating crowd, he untangles my hair from his waistcoat button. Shoved flat against his brown suit, his bulky body, my head little higher than his waist, I wait helplessly, without a murmur as he labours to free us both, tearing off some of the hair in the process.

All of this has taken so little time, or the crowd must have been so dense, that no one in my family even notices my panic. Neither do I feel a need to share it with anyone later. Especially since we have to escape the crowd as quickly as possible. Here and there the German soldiers are stopping people and asking for their papers. By the time we get home, the excitement of the train journey is behind me. There were new things to get used to in Budapest.

Our house, three streets from the Pest end of the Margaret Bridge, has been designated for Jews. A house with the yellow star. It means we are allowed to stay there, but we have to share our old apartment with four or five other families, each of them fatherless, since the men have been conscripted into the labour battalions now that the Germans have occupied Hungary.

"Are we really going to live with Ava and Vera in the next room? Wonderful!"

Ava and Vera are our cousins. In the past we have seen them only at birthday parties or during special family gatherings. For now, my excitement at "moving in together" like an endless children's party has overcome my fear of being snipped away.

4.

The next morning I stand at the window of our old dining room and watch German soldiers march in a solid block down Tatra Street. It's a sunny, bright day; I can see them perfectly. Their marching is heavy, relentless, and the heaviness of their step, their songs, and their dark uniforms grips my heart. Then I catch the look in my mother's eyes and for a moment see something in them I haven't seen before. She is afraid.

I cannot say exactly when the decision was made, or whether anyone even made a decision, but from that point on nobody in our family speaks German. Mother has always been keen for us to become fluent in it, and we have always had a German-speaking governess who couldn't speak Hungarian, but from now on no one expects us to utter a single word in German.

I'm disappointed not to see Grandfather. He would have rushed to greet us at the train station, but he was arrested the day the Germans came in and was kept in jail in Kistarcsa, as a hostage.

Hostage?

I remember this word from one of our playground games. There are two teams, and the purpose of the game is to capture as many hostages from the other team as possible. But why would an old man, my own grandfather, be kept as a hostage? I don't want to ask Mother; I don't want to bring back that anxious, pained look in her eyes. At any rate, as soon as we get home she busies herself cleaning the apartment. She also starts to cook for all of us—there are ten, often eleven people now in our apartment—and to bake sometimes late into the night. She will send all her baking to Grandfather as often as it is permitted.

5.

Soldiers.

When we were still in the mountains, in Matrafured, I once saw Hungarian soldiers waiting in a big hall, the air heavy with perspiration, the fumes from their cheap cigarettes, and the smell of coarse, wet khaki. They are sitting relaxed, chatting, waiting for their next orders. Outside, at the same time, I hear a band of wandering gypsies, happy and jeering, singing a cruel song:

Jew, Jew, stinking Jew,
What do you think you're doing here?
May you rot in your mother ...

The words are horrible, and so is the laughter that follows. I don't understand any of this at all. Everyone who looks at me or Sandy can see that we bathe, wash, and change our clothes. So does everyone in my family and everyone around me. The gypsies, on the other hand ... Well ... Doesn't everyone see that it's the gypsies who don't wash or wear clean clothes? One doesn't talk about these things, of course, and I would never remark about it in their presence. But why are they allowed to sing these horrible lies about us? And are those soldiers enjoying the songs? Are they merely indifferent or do they think the songs are funny?

Shy, unable to move, to breathe, I feel paralyzed by the sight of the soldiers. By any uniform. Yet only a few months ago I used to look at the kindly, impeccably dressed policeman on the street corner as someone who would protect me, whom I could turn to if I was lost or in trouble.

Back in Budapest it is getting difficult to tell who would help and who would just shrug his shoulders or even turn against me if I asked for help. The streetcar conductor, for example. There is no doubt in my mind that before we left Budapest for the mountains, both the conductor and the driver of the streetcar would have been protective, kindly. Sandy, for example, almost had a serious accident a year before the occupation. She was coming home with Tante, our governess, from her school in Buda. The conductor, not noticing that the woman and the child belonged together, rang the bell to signal the driver to continue. Sandy was already on the platform of the moving streetcar, while Tante was left behind on the sidewalk. All the passengers on the platform weren't able to hold Sandy back. She broke free and leapt off the moving streetcar. The driver stopped immediately. There was a big commotion; the streetcar could have killed her, or could have cut off her feet, but thank God she was unharmed except for some bruises on her knees.

That was a year ago, a year before the Germans marched in. Now, wearing the yellow star on my chest, I'm getting uneasy whenever we have to use the streetcar. What if the conductor deliberately rang off the car before Mother could mount the platform after us, and what if the driver did not want to help us? Now that I'm wearing the yellow star, I can no longer count on the good will of Uncle Driver or Uncle Conductor.

And wearing the yellow star means I cannot count on the kindness of the other passengers. And what would happen if the gypsies suddenly showed up and began singing their jeering song? Would the people without the star simply pretend they hadn't seen, hadn't heard? Would they even sing along? There's only one conclusion I can draw: since we have to wear the yellow star, we had better stay close to home, we had better not mix at all with those who don't have to wear it. We'd better not venture anywhere at all.

Of course, the yellow star and the Germans, and even Father away in the labour battalion, and Grandpa being kept as a hostage, are not on my mind all the time. Sandy and I visit the other children in the apartment house. In our apartment, the children are thick as thieves. There is feuding between my cousins and Sandy, but I get along with them well. Sandy also has showdowns with Ian, the husky, fair-haired boy of nine who lives with his mother in our former living room. Sandy has made it clear that if Ian wants to fight, she'll return it in kind. There's nothing ladylike about Sandy: she takes it for granted that she should be in command of the situation, and then relentlessly establishes her superiority. More than once, Ian has hit her and she's hit him right back, never mind Mother's edict that girls shouldn't fight with boys. Once Sandy determines that justice is on her side, she acknowledges no authority and recognizes no compromise.

Yet as different as we are in most things, in one thing Sandy, my eight-year-old older sister, and I agree absolutely: both of us would simply and categorically fight any attempt to separate us from our parents. We belong together. Or rather, since each of us belongs to our parents, we two must belong together as well.

Being separated from our parents now means something different to Sandy and me: being separated from Mother. Father has had to join a labour battalion, and although we see him whenever he can get a leave, we're no longer one with him. All the stronger, now, is our union with our mother. Mother, Sandy, and I—I think of the three of us as a single being. My hands hold on to Mother, and so do Sandy's. As long as we can touch her, be near her, hang on to her skirt, nothing else matters.

"We'll go anywhere to stay with you, Mummy," we tell her. "Nothing can make any difference to us as long as we're with you." We speak, think, breathe in unison with Sandy. Yet by October, when the Arrow Cross Party takes over, the adults are trying to explain to us that some time in the future a separation may become necessary. Sandy and I may be placed with a Christian family in the countryside—it may be easier to hide this way. We may even have to be sent abroad with some kind of children's transport to the West. Both Father and Mother have at times been serious about these possibilities. There's even a hint of our joining Auntie Mimi and Uncle Isa, who are among the very few fortunate ones. The ones who have been able to buy their way out of the country, to Switzerland or overseas by a special transport.

6.

I remember Auntie Mimi and her husband coming to visit the family at Grandmother Betty's apartment at the beginning of summer. They arrive escorted by a soldier in khaki with a red armband on his sleeve and a hollow smile on his face. (That smile makes me shudder, then ponder endlessly.) The family assembles in Grandmother's sitting room. Grandmother is an old lady of seventy; she lives here with Uncle Frank. He is a chemical engineer like our father, but he looks quite unlike our jovial, hefty Father. Uncle Frank has a narrow face and a slim build; his left side was paralyzed by the Spanish flu he contracted in 1920. Every time we arrive for our weekly visit he has a serene smile on his thin, curved lips.

He enjoys drawing out his two little nieces in conversation, but his words, even his jokes, are always gentle, careful not to embarrass or offend. Sometimes I feel like helping him by lifting his game leg so that he can turn in his armchair, or by pushing his helpless left arm toward the glass of water or toward the pen he may want to reach on his desk, but I don't dare touch him. I approach his green velvet armchair shyly at the beginning of our visit, when I offer my face to be kissed. Yet I enjoy staying close to him, his serenity and silence.

Grandmother Betty has something like a moustache. She used to be quite a beauty, I hear with some astonishment—famous for her straight carriage and beautiful, clean features all over the city of Munkacs. Although I know Munkacs is my father's birthplace, I ponder deeply about that beauty. Could an old lady like Grandma ever have been beautiful? She is always well groomed, her short, white hair under a hairnet, her compact body clad in dark grey or navy blue, always a sombre, heavy fabric. Yet I'm somehow reluctant to approach her because she would pinch my cheeks after I kissed her and insist on an "Eskimo kiss," which always ends with us rubbing our noses together. I don't find this ritual funny, perhaps because I don't really know her well enough, or I simply suspect that she isn't really cheerful when trying to go through this comic ritual.

There is no doubt, however, that Grandmother Betty is part of the stable order around me, ready to offer protection or warmth when things aren't going well. I remember, for example, that at Sandy's six-year birthday party, it was she who saved me from what I thought was to be a horrible death from suffocating.

Mother had put on a big production for Sandy's birthday. There were many, many children, each invited to choose a character from *Snow White*, and Mother had supplied masks and elaborate costumes for all of us. We were to act out the story, which most of us already knew from the Walt Disney film and from its book version. Snow White, of course, was played by the birthday girl herself. Sandy's dark hair shone like ebony, although her eyes were doelike, not blue, light blue like mine (but I would be too shy and too young to play Snow White). There's no doubt that Sandy was a convincing princess. The children, all masked and costumed, kept milling around her in ever-increasing frustration and then, unmistakably, boredom. Somehow the drama wasn't materializing around her. Each and every one of us knew the story well, but Sandy knew the whole *book*—line by line, word for word. Never did she think she should refrain from correcting every line or not interfere with the way the other children wanted to act out the story. One by one, the

Memories of Sandy's sixth birthday party

hunter, the prince, the dwarfs, the reindeer, the rabbits, and even the little birds who were to sing while Snow White was baking her pie, were giving up in quiet desperation.

Or perhaps the party came to a standstill because of the photographers. They were professionals invited for this special occasion and were having the children pose for group photos and portraits. I remember getting more and more disoriented and tired of it all. But more hurtful than anything else was that in the awkward costume and behind the rigid mask of Dopey, I couldn't move or see and after a while couldn't breathe. The air was getting unbearably hot inside the wax-and-enamel mask. Blindly I felt my way toward a cluster of adults, crying, or rather whimpering for anyone's attention. It was Grandmother who came to the rescue by removing my mask—I would never have understood what was to be done—cutting open the holes for the eyes, enlarging the slit for the mouth. Of course, the character of Dopey must have been quite appropriate for my dopeyness, and the adults around Grandmother smiled in amusement at my misery.

But now, receiving Auntie Mimi, her youngest daughter, Grandmother Betty probably doesn't even see me. Around her thin, curved mouth are two bitter lines down to the chin, and her lips are trembling.

The family is assembled to pray to our forefathers to bless us, their children and grandchildren, survivors of the departed. I recognize the name of my paternal grandfather, Joseph. I never met him, for he died years before I was born. Nevertheless, I know him from photographs; a gentle, rounded face, a domed forehead surrounded by a crown of fine, snow-white hair. What we are praying for, Mother explains to me in a whisper, is that he and the forefathers intercede for us all—especially, at this moment, for Auntie Mimi and her husband.

"To intercede?"

"To step closer to God and pray for us."

But wherever the forefathers may be, there is something quite clear: we are praying for Mimi and her husband as they prepare to undertake a long, long journey. They are about to leave for a safe space, somewhere in Switzerland or America. I don't know where these places are, except that they are both far away. I also understand that it's a good thing they are able to go and that the family has to be grateful they have the opportunity.

Yet there must also be some kind of a danger here, because not only Grandmother, but also the usually serene Uncle Frank and Auntie Rosie, are grim and anxious. Somehow, although nobody mentions this, I understand that for some reason we may never see them again.

Overseas.

What is over the sea?

I see a huge ship with three big masts in front of my eyes, surrounded by light green waves. The waves are crested with white foam. There is a white spray around the ship and a milky white mist against the transparent pink sky. The word "overseas" evokes one of the oil paintings in our lavish living room, a picture in an ornate gilded frame, a seascape with tiny dots suggesting a multitude of people among the sails. But now I don't see any of these people, only the terrible tearing away as the ship is pulling away from the harbour, getting smaller and smaller against the windswept pink sky.

There is crying and praying among the adults, and we all embrace one another. Yet in spite of all these emotions, I cannot take my eyes off the soldier at the entrance to the apartment. Is he here to protect Auntie and Uncle, or is he their guard and they his prisoners? And is he going to take us all, if we cry or even pray too loud?

The adults are subdued, and embrace in tears. I sense that Father and Auntie Rosie are trying to control themselves in front of the soldier. I can also feel that they want to act cheerful and confident so that their Mummy won't feel anxious about losing her youngest daughter. Father is trying to smile, but his deep-set, light brown eyes with the dark eyelashes are dimmed with tears. I'm sad for all of them, but there is also excitement in the air. What if some day I were to leave with a transport. Overseas?

Of course, I don't want to go if it means leaving all my relatives behind. But Father, Mother, Sandy, and I are one body; if worst came to worst, the four of us could still survive as a family. If it came to that.

But to part from Mother and go with Sandy? Or to go by myself? That thought is unthinkable. My parents and Sandy—they are me, part of me, they are like the air I breathe.

"But can't you see, my dear," Mother says, "you might have a better chance if you were to leave first. Of course, we would find a way to come after you, to join you ..."

Both Sandy and I cry and argue vehemently.

"It doesn't matter where we are, how little we have to eat, how small the place where we have to hide—we'll never separate from you."

There's a tiny washroom in our apartment, a room three by five at most. I speculate how we could stay there in hiding, the four of us, if need be, if we arranged our feet and limbs just so. (Whenever I see a public phone booth, the dimensions present an irresistible challenge for me to sort out body positions for two adults and two children in case of emergency.)

7.

"Nicht für dem Kindern"—"Not for the children." The adults huddle together as I approach. The unmistakable signal of their worry: they have changed the subject of their conversation. There's no mistaking the telling glances: this is not for the children to hear.

Not that I mind being protected from what they are talking about. In fact, I'm grateful for being sheltered, protected. I've grown afraid of the sound of certain words as much as what they describe. Words can hurt to be heard. "Snipped off ... Cut off ..." The cutting away of my hand from my mother's, the tearing away of my body while I'm hanging on to her skirt.

And I also know when you have to keep certain words from others. I'm quite aware of the vulnerability of adults, and I pity them for their afflictions. Especially for the affliction of being adults and not having the shelter of their parents' body hovering over them any more.

I vividly see myself—I can't be more than three—standing in the corner of our nursery, a large, green, sunny room on the third floor with cast-iron bars on the window so that we children don't fall out when we aren't being watched. I must have just graduated from the crib to the bed, because I can see quite clearly the L-shaped bed I share with Sandy. The wallpaper is bright yellow with colourful balloons and children tumbling all over them. I'm standing in the corner, facing the built-in closet with its door painted the same light green as the rest of the furniture.

To have to stand in the corner is a great humiliation. After a fit of crying, I'm still shaking with the bitter injustice of the punishment. One is being made to suffer more, simply because one has already been suffering. And then, bit by bit, even though I'm still rigid with anger and defiance, the cloud of bitterness rises from my chest, slowly wafts from me. Suddenly I feel the rain clouds of pity and sorrow shift from myself to the pitiable adult, Tante, our elegant blond governess, who is slowly emerging in front of my eyes, pulled down from her superhuman height in her starched white smock by my single, simple thought: "The poor woman, she no longer has her Mummy."

Without coercion I turn from the green corner of my exile to ask forgiveness. Not because I have to, not because she broke my spirit but because of the warm, revitalizing pity that now overflows my heart: "Look at that poor adult creature who no longer has a Mummy. How I must love her."

I'm also well aware of the vulnerability even of apparently robust figures like Grandfather, Mother's father. He's tall, big-boned, with the body of an athlete, a soldier, a farmer. He can walk miles and miles for his own amusement, and when I wake up early, I watch him in the bathroom splashing cold water on his face, neck, and chest, then scrubbing his reddened skin vigorously with a sponge. Then he rubs his muscular torso with a rough towel, and only then is he ready to put on the crisp, perfectly ironed fine linen shirt he has carefully laid out for himself. Only after this grooming ritual is he ready to join us, his grandchildren, and Tante at the breakfast table, which has been laid out for the four of us in the nursery. While we're having our cocoa and toast, or bread and butter with jam, he's feasting on bacon with red paprika all around the skin, and a huge chunk of fresh brown bread. With a pocket knife, he's cutting the bacon into tiny pieces and cutting little cubes of bread to go with it. And to go with his hearty peasant breakfast, he has a tot of rum in his tea— a large tot, I don't doubt. He eats meticulously but with so much gusto that I overhear Tante muttering under her breath: "like a peasant."

Though he's lived forty-odd years in the metropolis, one can still tell that Grandpa was raised in the country. One can hear it on his Lowland accent and in the gusto with which he chooses his words. There is nothing like going on a hike with Grandpa. He isn't the city-bred tourist posing as a mountain climber. Unlike other well-to-do Jewish merchants reluctantly taking their weekend exercise, Grandfather is at home in the forest. He knows about brooks and trees, and he can tell us which berries are poisonous and which are safe to eat. He builds campfires quickly and without a fuss, and when I grow tired, he carries me on his shoulders for miles without the slightest effort. Yet I also know he must be looked after carefully. When Grandma died, something broke inside him, and we children both sense that we must never, ever withhold our love from him, for if we did he would have nothing left to live for.

No one in the family has ever told me this in so many words, but it's clear to me that I must never turn away my face when he picks me up to kiss me on his return from work in the afternoon. So many hours after his morning shave, his beard bristles hard as he brushes his face against mine in hearty greeting. Once when I pulled my face away, I saw the hurt in his blue-grey eyes and felt ashamed.

When I was five (how far away that time is now, almost a year ago, before the Germans came), I broke Cini, the beautiful old porcelain doll with her blushing cheeks, the doll that belonged to Mother when she was little. I knew I had done something terrible, and I cried without cease over the broken shards that had been her sweet, dimpled face. Grandfather tried to comfort me:

"What's the matter, why are you crying so, my little one?"

Suddenly I knew I wasn't really crying about the broken doll or about the possibility of punishment. "It's for Granny I'm crying. That she died and I'll never see her again." And now my tears could flow unchecked, drawn out by the gentle mist in Grandfather's eyes. "What a lovely, tender child," he must have thought, and how happy he must have been that I shared his grief.

Grandfather's vulnerability is obvious to me, in spite of his rough talk and rustic appearance. I'm proud he's my Grandpa. On October 15, the day the Hungarian Nazi Party, the Arrow Cross, takes over, he organizes a guard in our apartment building—one of several houses in our neighbourhood with the yellow star above the entrance. There are no young or middle-aged men in the house—all the husbands are away in the labour battalions, and some of them have already been taken out of the country. There are only women, children, and elderly people in the house, four to six families crowded into each formerly elegant middle-class apartment. All of us are Jewish except for the Szucses, our caretakers.

Having heard that the terrorists have taken over the government, Grandfather has the heavy wooden gate of the house shut, and he stands guard with an axe in the corner. He'd been a soldier in the Great War and had spent four years in the trenches. If the Arrow Cross boys want to enter, he won't give us up gently.

8.

But after a night of anxious expectations, we're relieved to find that this particular building has been spared for now. Nevertheless, by the next morning, it's been decided that we in this apartment will leave the Jewish house and go into hiding. Father by then has joined his labour battalion, so the decision must have been made by Grandfather and the four women. Grandfather, Mother, Sandy and I, our two cousins, Ava and Veronica, and their mother will go together. Joining us will be Mrs. Dautsch and her son. Mrs. Dautsch's cousin, Susan, and her one-year-old baby will have to find another hiding place. I'm surprised to learn that we'll be joined by Mr. Kis, a balding, middle-aged bachelor. It's he who has found the hiding place for us—a room with a washroom behind another apartment in a house near the Amusement Park. The new house doesn't have the yellow star, so the Arrow Cross will be less likely to search it for Jews. Mr. Kis is a friend of Mrs. Dautsch, a strong, handsome woman of twenty-nine or thirty—Mother's age. Her husband was taken to the Russian Front with one of the Jewish labour battalions several months ago.

Mr. Kis must have known there would be five children coming along, yet he seems unprepared for the reality of our presence. The small room seems crammed with us, and the women are desperate to keep us all silent, not to reveal to the outside world that there is life in the little room behind the apartment. It's hard to keep us absolutely silent, to make us act as if we don't exist. I remember standing by our window, looking out at the grey sky, and tracing icy tulip petals with my fingernail on the frosty glass.

"Come away, quick, duck now!" Mother pulls me away quickly in alarm. What if someone had seen me standing there just now? And what if someone saw my tulip on the windowpane? Something as insignificant as that could give us all away.

Mother makes us recite stories to one another very, very quietly. I know a long, long story, all in verse, of Latyi Matyi, the comic pastry cook who has been the children's clown hero in Budapest for the past few years. I recite the story with great enjoyment, being proud of myself for knowing it all by heart. A whole book of poetry, and full of jokes. But we also have to be very careful about our laughter.

Then, just as the women are growing tired of entertaining us, and Mr. Kis is beginning to resent our restlessness, Grandfather takes over. Sandy and I and Ian and our two cousins gather round as he embarks on his meandering, never-ending, always exciting story about the young vagabond Frankie the Magnificent. Sandy and I had Grandfather write down Frankie's adventures for us many long months ago, and now we greet him as our long-lost friend.

But despite all our efforts to stay quiet, after a long, tense week the care-taker tells Mr. Kis that the hiding place has been noticed. Some of the tenants may already be watching us, and we must leave the premises immediately. But how can we leave quickly without being seen? For three women, five children, and two men it isn't easy to stir without making a commotion.

The janitor keeps watch and signals to Mr. Kis when we should leave, group by group in quick succession. For now we have to go to the top floor and take shelter in the laundry room. After sunset we'll be able to leave the house without being seen.

The laundry room, on the sixth floor, is a bleak, unfurnished room with exposed metal pipes. In better days the washerwomen would have done the laundry in huge wooden tubs against the bare walls, the exposed metal pipes, and the huge tanks of water. There are of course no seats. We sit on our bags or bundles, or simply crouch on the floor when we get tired. I stand next to a small high-set window, looking out. The grey-blue cirrus clouds are moving across the sky lazily. I'm watching figures pass by in the clouds. Grandfather crouches beside me so that our heads are at the same level. He sees the same floating figures as I do. We describe them to each other: the angels, the leaping lions, the haggard old women in their mysterious flowing capes, the wild heroes on horseback, slowly dissolving figures in flight ...

There is magic in seeing the same figures in the clouds with someone else. And of course, the way Grandfather describes them, the figures are somehow more real. And there is another thing: listening to his calm, deep voice so close beside me, my fear has receded. It's still there somewhere, but it is our collective fear. It cannot single me out, it cannot take me over.

But after a while we can't see the clouds anymore. In November, after five o'clock it is getting darker by the moment. On our way upstairs to the laundry room we are warned by the janitor to watch out for a man living on the fifth floor. He's such a vigilant follower of the Arrow Cross that he wouldn't march even to the common toilet without his gun on his shoulder.

As soon as it grows dark, we begin winding our way down the staircase. Grandfather goes ahead. On the fifth floor he bumps into a young man. He must be the one. There's a gun on his shoulder, and on his arm he wears the red, white, and green band of the Arrow Cross.

"Good evening to you," Grandfather stops him, offering heartfelt greetings in his deep, Lowland dialect.

The young man returns the greeting politely. By folk custom, they call each other "My Uncle" and "My Younger Brother." Grandpa knows well the intricacies of small talk. Crops, rain, war, hard times, hopes for a good future. Just from the hearty, even timbre of his voice, we understand that we're to leave quietly, calmly, while we're protected by the screen of the two men's friendly conversation.

It's a long way down from the sixth floor, and we should make no noise. No noise. Yet I fear that walking on tiptoe will give me away if anyone sees me. (The trick, I tell myself, is to put down the sole of my shoe without letting the heel touch the stairs.) We're moving down the dark staircase silently, furtively. The group disperses, unit by unit.

Mother, Grandpa, Sandy, and I remain together. Damjanich Street is dark—a streetlight here and there, but all I can see are rings of fog around the bases of the dark, cold metal lampposts. The shafts of light break into but don't quite penetrate the fog. Still, in the dimness of one streetlight I recognize a familiar figure in a short jacket and a visor cap. Even in this light, I know the cap is beige and grey.

Everything about him is beige and grey, even his moustache and his heavy, expressionless face. It's Mr. Szucs, our janitor. Somehow, during this long and eventful day, Mr. Szucs has been sent for. Somehow, a messenger must have been found—Grandpa must have given him money. And now he is here, waiting for us.

Our house with the yellow star is more than an hour's walk. Mr. Szucs will walk ahead of us; we're under his protection. If we're stopped, we should say we're his relatives from the country.

Standing under the deep, foggy sky, Sandy and I are leaning against Mother in her dark overcoat. Her black silk kerchief with the red roses is knotted tightly under her chin and pulled down to her forehead to cast a shadow over her face, over her strong, hooked nose. Grandfather is standing across the sidewalk in his heavy mauve overcoat, his angular wide-brimmed hat casting a shadow over his eyes. He leans forward to embrace Mother, and automatically I raise my face to him for a kiss. Suddenly I realize that he is not to come with us. Just then, almost imperceptibly, Mother backs away, stiff with anxiety.

"Don't, Dad, don't," she whispers. "Don't draw attention to us."

Grandpa steps back and slowly but decisively turns away. He walks away from us in his heavy overcoat with wide shoulder pads, in the shadow of his broad-brimmed hat. We follow him with our eyes until the fog and the darkness swallow him. He's going to another hiding place, by himself.

Mr. Szucs signals us: it's time to start. The three of us follow at a distance. We follow him cautiously in the dark, foggy night, huddled near our mother, keeping close to the walls along the sidewalk. None of us will see Grandfather again.

9.

Following Mr. Szucs, we get back to our apartment house. To my surprise, it is no longer a house with a yellow star. We're no longer allowed to live there at all. Right now, we have to be extremely careful because various gentiles, members of the Arrow Cross or people with connections to it, are eager to move into the newly vacated Jewish apartments. Although our apartment has not yet been occupied, it's not advisable to stay here for long. Mr. Szucs indicates that he has been taking chances for our sake: he has been interrogated and slapped around by some members of the Arrow Cross who suspect him of being friendly with Jews. The name for such a person is "Jewish hireling," and the punishment for being one is death. We understand that we can't count on him in the future, whatever arrangements my parents had made with him before the occupation.

In the meantime, Father must have learned that we're back from our hiding place and in need of another. He has already prepared for this contingency. Once more, someone has acted as messenger (and been generously paid for it). Early in the morning we set out again, each of us carrying a handbag, to meet Father on the boulevard. I'm given to understand that though we are to meet him, we must pretend not to recognize him.

We meet him on St. Stephen Boulevard on our way to the convent on Hermina Road on the outskirts of the city. He's wearing his labour battalion uniform—untailored, creased khaki fatigues and jacket and a khaki doughboy cap that doesn't fit him. He's accompanied by a Hungarian soldier in army uniform, who wears a special armband to indicate that he is escorting a Jew on leave from the labour battalion.

Mother, Sandy, and I are to follow the two men from a distance. We aren't wearing our yellow stars today. No one has explained this to me, but deep down I know we could all be shot if we're caught without the yellow star. Wearing it, of course, we could not leave our district. As before, Mother has pulled her black silk scarf down over her brow, and for now she has bent her head—"May the shadow of the scarf keep my nose in darkness," she must be praying. And I'm praying too, while rehearsing my role. If anyone should stop us, I'm to say: "My name is Eva Steinbach. Praised be our Lord, Jesus Christ." I'm not sure why, but the greeting with Jesus Christ's name has an exciting ring to it. With pride and a sense of my own importance, I add my own name to the greeting.

I feel that I should pray for this journey to end quickly, very quickly. From time to time, despite our hurry, Father turns back to look at us. He can't repress a boyish smile and winks at us with good humour.

"Sandy looks too much like me for me ever to deny that she's my daughter," he tells us when we come within hearing distance.

With stiff, nervous gestures, Mother signals for him to move ahead. We mustn't draw attention to ourselves. We have to move quickly, pretend to be invisible.

"Just act calm, as if we're going about our day's business. As if we're above suspicion."

The weather is crisp and clear, the sun is up—everybody can see us clearly. I feel desperate that I can't turn invisible at will.

Fortunately, the streets are deserted as we move toward the outskirts. After another half-hour's brisk walk, Father stops to watch us enter the gate of a large grey rectangular building. The grounds of the convent are not extensive, but to me, the building with its classical façade looks formidable. There is a porta, a formal entrance with a porter's lodge (how long could we hide in there, the three of us, in an emergency?), which leads to a dark hall and corridors behind it. The smell is unusual: clean, quaint, intriguing (the smell of soap, cooked cabbage, and incense, I soon learn). I'm expecting someone to come up to me, bend down, and ask me a question so that I'll have a chance to deliver the greeting I have been practising. "My name is Eva Steinbach. Praise to our Lord, Jesus Christ." But no one seems to notice me at all.

It takes quite a while before I realize that the building behind the six-foot brick wall is the barracks of Father's labour battalion. That is where he learned from his comrades that the nuns were hiding Jewish women and children. Somehow he made contact and arranged to get us into the convent.

What I can't understand at all is how Father managed to do anything for us here. No man is allowed onto the grounds of the convent, ever. My deepest grievance against the nuns is that Father is never able to speak to us or visit us inside the building. He climbs over the wall whenever he can, and we sneak out to the courtyard to be with him for a few moments. But he has to be careful that no one but the guard he has bribed sees him leave. And we have to worry that the nuns may throw him out because he is a man.

Father is capable of acting as our breadwinner and provider even in these adverse circumstances. One day he brings us four crisp, freshly baked rolls, spread thick with butter and honey. Wading deep in the fallen leaves between the brick wall and the grey walls of the convent, we huddle together, all four of us, savouring the delicious gold-filled rolls. I'm huddling between Mother and Father with my sister, munching, chewing, licking the rolls, the butter, the honey—savouring this delightful, forbidden moment for all it's worth. At that moment I am more than ecstatic: I am deeply content.

But only a few days after the day of the rolls and honey, at dawn while she is in the bathroom, my mother hears a commotion from the direction of the barracks. Sharp voices are shouting commands. Men are scurrying around in groups Then she hears shots being fired, and it seems to her that she can hear the cracking of twigs on our side of the brick wall. The battalion is being rounded up after several months in the city: the men are called into action. That means they're about to be marched to the front and to almost certain death from the cold, starvation, enemy bullets, and the cruelty of their Hungarian commanding officers. Although I don't ask for an explanation at the time, I remember overhearing in the summer that Paul Gergely, our jovial, long-time banker friend, committed suicide after he learned that his battalion was about to leave the country. He had had heart trouble for years, and he found it easier to swallow cyanide than to face the ordeal.

Later in the day, Mother finds out that the shots she heard had been aimed at Father. At the last minute he had escaped over the brick wall onto the grounds of the convent. At the entrance he asked the nuns' permission to say goodbye to Mother. The nuns refused to admit him— no man was to enter the convent. Ever. But they did let him leave through another door, one that the Arrow Cross was not watching, and later they let Mother know he had been there and that he was well at the time. They also told her that the shot had grazed his pants, or perhaps they had been torn in jumping. Apart from that, he was unscathed. And he was on the run.

10.

The nuns. Mother understands their concern with rules, and she makes it clear to us that there is no use arguing about it. We had said our good-bye to Father a few days before the shots—we'd met behind the convent building. That was the first time I had ever seen Father cry. He had always been smiling, belittling Mother's fears and anxieties. When he led us to the convent, his mischievous backward glances showed unshakable family pride and an almost boyish confidence in himself and in us, that we were going to make it. After we returned to Budapest from Gyongyos, Father had been able to live with us for a short time before being called up to his labour battalion. In our whole house, he was the only one who never showed any signs of fear during an air raid. First you would hear the warning siren, then the janitor would sound the gong in the small, paved yard. As the siren grew louder and louder, so would the gong, until the tenants of the six-storey building fled to the cellar with their packages and bundles. The way I remember, those raids always took place at night, while we were sleeping. Mother always made sure we went to bed in our housecoats, socks, and tie-on slippers. She also had our coats and other necessities arranged in bundles for each of us to grab the moment the alarm sounded. We would stagger down, still half asleep, the two storeys to the main floor and down the narrow stairs to the dank, airless cellar.

Mother had us so perfectly prepared for these times that Sandy at eight and I at six were even able to help some of the older women with their packages while we descended the staircase, groping our way along the yellow elevator shaft. No lights were allowed whatsoever. Even with the blackout—the black paper pasted over the staircase windows—no candles could be lit until everyone was safely down.

Father's preparations for air raids were always haphazard. He was always next to us at those times, always a soothing, encouraging presence. He would keep telling Mother in his deep, gentle voice: "Stay calm, don't worry, rest calm, my dear! Rest easy, there's nothing to worry about. Not to worry, my dearest."

Only when we got to the crossing at the backyard could we catch a glimpse of one another in the pale moonlight. Father in bare feet, his bathrobe flopping open over his pyjamas. He had not even bothered to bring a belt, let alone his shoes or slippers or his allotted bag. Yet he was always cheerful and tranquil—anything to minimize our own alarm.

"We're only here as an exercise, a rehearsal," he would emphasize. "This doesn't mean anything at all. Why would anyone think we're in danger?"

But now, at our last meeting behind the convent walls, he embraces and kisses Mother, who is in tears. He embraces Sandy and me as well, patting us on the back, not talking to us. We know we're saying goodbye; we know that this time we're truly being separated. He doesn't talk because he doesn't want to cry, but Mother is sobbing unashamedly, clinging to him. For once, even Father cannot laugh it away: his features are distorted as if in anger; but no, he is unmistakably crying. Father and Mother embrace once more, for a long time, then he tears himself away. Still crying, without words, he waves to us slowly as he walks away.

We cling to Mother. I want to hide in her, but also to console her. Both Sandy and I hold on to her tight, not relaxing our grip until she slowly, gradually collects herself. I make a mental note that tonight I must pray to God very distinctly, repeating Father's name, his full name, several times and very clearly so that God will not possibly overlook him as his special ward from now on. Although I turn to God with my wishes or fears several times each day, it has never occurred to me that there is a better time for special prayers than in the evening, which is when we've been taught to say our prayers. "When I close my eyes in the evening, dear God please look after me and my parents, my sister, my grandfather ..." The list is long, and then I repeat the especially important parts several times after.

But for now, Mother is ready to go on with reading our story, and for a while I forget everything else. She's reading to us about Little Lord Fauntleroy, a story that seems to follow us not only through the bombardments, but also through the otherwise unbearable moments when we're on the run or in hiding. Whenever we settle down around her to listen to the story, whether in the cellar amidst the hysterical screaming of women and children, or during the whizzing and then the deadly silence of the airplanes, or in a quiet corner of our dormitory in the convent, the world simply disappears for me completely. Only a few minutes after Father's departure, after the wrenching feeling of seeing him cry for the first time, and of seeing him walk away from us sobbing, I am ready to shed tears for Little Lord Fauntleroy who had to leave his sweet, gentle mother behind in America. And I am deeply delighted that he is going to England to meet his strict but exceedingly rich, mysterious grandfather. A real lord, living in his own castle.

The zooming, booming sound of the approaching airplanes, the deafening silence before they release their burden, and the wheezing, whistling, earth-shattering detonation. If it is far enough away, we are safe for the time being. If we are covered by plaster, or hear the noise of falling objects, and feel the tremor of the walls, it fell close by but we are still safe. As long as we can hear the noise and feel our limbs, it is all right, we've gotten away. Until it's time for the next round. The approaching planes, their hovering over us in a moment of breathless silence, and then the sounds of explosions. There's a little girl in the corner, named Lydia. She keeps wailing hysterically. Her mother is trying in vain to calm her. But in our corner of the cellar life has stood still. Mother puts her arms around us and goes on with our story.

11.

In the daytime, in the convent, the nuns are hovering in the background. I look at them with admiration, and then, after I hear that they did not let in Father on the day of the shooting, I look at them askance. Mother is matter-of-fact about them. They do what they do because of the rules of their religion. They follow the rules, not necessarily their hearts. There is only one nun who lights up my mother's eyes when she approaches, indeed, whenever she is mentioned. She's a middle-aged woman with moist, dark eyes and a warm, gentle smile. She's not the Mother Superior (Kind Mother in Hungarian), but she seems to be greatly respected by the others. The children simply adore her. Mother calls her "Mater Dolorosa" and says she reminds her of the gentle, suffering Madonna she has seen in paintings. To me the words simply mean Sister Rosa. She occasionally talks to the children in her deep, melodious voice, and somehow her glance is warmer and more real than that of the other nuns. But we don't see a great deal of her because she is in charge of a bevy of novitiates—young girls who are training to become nuns. One of them, a shy and beautiful girl of fifteen with heavy blond braids, is called Maria. Rumour has it she is actually a Jewish orphan. She has a shy smile and smooth, soft skin and I wish she would notice me and talk to me. But she only smiles at us from a distance.

Sister Rosa—Dolorosa—is the only one Mother feels enthusiastic about. There is something about this middle-aged woman's expression that takes Mother back to her early days in convent school. In those days, the greater her fear of the strict nun-teachers, the greater her tenderness and gratitude toward the ones who took pity on her, who sometimes paid attention to her. Mother is blatantly skeptical toward any kind of bigotry, or even piety, but she had experienced the mysterious attraction of religion as a child and as an adolescent. At the age of six I don't understand much about Mother's life, yet I'm absorbing almost by osmosis some of her complicated distinctions between the other nuns, who perform their rituals as a duty, and Sister Rosa, who somehow feels and lives her religion.

12.

By now we've been hiding in the convent for six weeks. On a mild day in early December I wake with a scratchy feeling in my throat: I've developed a dry, hacking cough that brings tears to my eyes. We're walking on the grounds, Mother, Sandy, and I, in the company of Mrs. Jonalsky and a number of other women and children. Rather casually, it seems to me, we walk past a barn at the back of the grounds, and still casually, we stop to inspect it from within: it's a small, empty building with a thick layer of straw on the floor. The straw and the dust aggravate my cough, and I remember Mother telling me casually:

"Well, my dear, I hope you won't have a cough like that if we ever have to hide here."

Just then, as if on cue, we see the beautiful fifteen-year-old novice, Maria, running toward us from the porter's lodge, her long, thick braids flying behind her:

"They're here, the Arrow Cross! They're here!"

(Even today I remember that feeling of shock. "Not now, not now, I'm not prepared! I'll accept it later, but wait! I need time!" Long after, when I had an accident and needed emergency surgery, that is what I kept telling myself, angrily, helplessly: "Why don't you give me time? All that I'm asking is a bit of time! I want to prepare.")

All of us—five or six mothers and about ten children—rush back to the barn and bury ourselves in the straw as deeply as we can. The smell and the dryness irritate my throat. I struggle not to, but I erupt in a fit of coughing.

"Throw her out, silence her, strangle her—she'll give us all away," hisses Mrs. Jonalsky, raising her head above her two clinging daughters.

Mother pats my back reassuringly and searches her handbag for something to soothe my throat. She finds only a small piece of chocolate. I try to collect the saliva in my mouth, try to swallow hard, desperate to make my coughing subside for a while. By now Mrs. Jonalsky has stopped insisting that I be thrown out, even when I break into a new coughing fit. She must realize there is no way to get rid of me without drawing attention to the group, endangering us even further. And my mother's wordless contempt is enough to make her stop suggesting someone strangle me. Her hysteria turns into an intermittent hissing sound whenever I make a noise.

In the background we hear noises, voices shouting orders, bursts of loud cries, the shuffling of feet. Under the straw I hold my breath, lying close against my mother's body, and pray to be able to breathe without coughing. I don't want to visualize the things going on outside. As if trying to stop seeing them in my imagination, I squeeze my eyes shut, just like before going to sleep.

I've learned to dread the images that come to me in my dreams or while I'm trying to go to sleep. And to dread the words that jump into my head. So I murmur under my breath a long catalogue of things, of earthly delights. I list to myself all the favourite toys that used to be mine and all the things I'm going to do with them once the war is over and we move back to our home and I get back my toys. Judy, my India-rubber doll with her smart leather valise full of clothes, complete with tiny coat hangers, and the neat little drawers in the valise for her shoes and underwear, and the hard leather valise just big enough for her to fit in, is one of my favourite daydreams. Now, in my imagination, I obsessively arrange and rearrange her clothes.

I also conjure up the enormous doll's house Mother had built for me—for me alone—when I had to stay home for six weeks with scarlet fever. I make a mental list of each little room, each piece of furniture, the dishes, the plates, the food I'm going to bake for my dolls, and of course for the rest of us too, as soon as the war is over. It's very important to recite the catalogue carefully and several times, as fast as possible. If I fall asleep in the middle of the catalogue, perhaps I will dream about my favourite dolls, Judy's clothes, and the tiny hangers. Go on, go on, go on.

I'm afraid of fear. The images are clamouring to break in shouting those terrible words: *Snipped off. Transport. Jewish hireling. Slapped around. Deportations. Cattle cars.* All the horrible words I've overheard and don't quite understand and daren't ask about. But there are also the pictures of things I've actually seen. The frightening poster of the little girl with the big blue eyes. I should never have looked at it though it's posted all over the walls, even in the rubble of the bomb craters. A little girl holding a broken doll. But what is most horrible is what happened to her hand. The fingers are bleeding, and some of them are torn off ... The hand is mutilated ... The poster is a warning to the Christian population: "Don't let your children pick up dolls thrown down from the airplanes: they are ploys of the Jewish world conspiracy. The dolls are explosives. The Jews are conspiring a painful death for your children."

I don't fully understand the words on the poster, but I know there is a remarkable resemblance between me and the little girl. Other people have noticed, too. I can't bear to think of her mutilated, bleeding hand ... I can't bear to see it. Yet when I close my eyes before going to sleep, often I cannot help myself, I have to see it.

"Judy, John, my favourite dollies, and the dishes and clothes ..." I whisper my catalogue desperately as I cling to Mother.

I don't feel the tension in her body, only her warmth through her coarse, unlined woollen coat. Then I doze off. I must have, because although I still know the coat is dark green, I really can't see colours anymore: darkness has fallen outside. I hear distant noises and see lights glimmering, and then everything dies down.

"They must have left," the women whisper among themselves.

Under the straw, we don't dare make the slightest move. Then suddenly, unmistakably, nearby, we hear a man's footsteps. He's approaching, closer and closer. He's *here*. The barn door suddenly swings open and a shaft of light falls on our crouching bodies.

Light is exposure. Light is nakedness. Light is unendurable, like the rigid pain of shame. To sink into the straw, into the earth! My body has turned rigid, lifeless. All I feel is a sinking sensation; the blood is draining from my head, from my body. I have ceased to breathe, have already ceased to live. There is a raw, hot pull in my stomach, a tightening, gnawing, nauseous ecstasy. I'm going to die. Waves of cold and then waves of dry electric heat run over my body in staccato motion.

Then suddenly, Mother's stiff body comes alive beside me. I understand nothing yet, but I feel that all is well. I open my eyes: the shaft of light is the gardener's small pocket light. The Arrow Cross men have left, and the gardener is on our side. He comes to fetch us: quickly, we can now return to the convent.

My limbs are numb, my breath uneven as we get up in the dark to get back into the building. We enter through the back entrance and are ushered into a darkened room behind the refectory. The nuns have a stage here with a curtain for student shows and concerts. The backstage area is full of boxes and old clothes.

A few nuns in their white habits are waiting for us. They help us get ready. We must prepare quickly.

"You must go. You have to go right away. Please go—go quickly."

Bit by bit we find out what just happened. In vain, Sister Rosa stood in front of the children, her arms spread to protect them from the soldiers. The Arrow Cross men pushed her aside and took away all the mothers and children. They also threatened all the nuns with cruel punishment for hiding Jews on the premises. They promised Sister Rosa they would be back to catch anyone still hiding and told her they would be keeping the convent under constant surveillance from now on. They demanded her word that there were no longer, nor would there ever be again, any more Jewish women and children in the convent. She was silent. They told her that even though she was a nun, the next time she would not escape the torture and death due to any ordinary Jewish hireling. She kept silent. Finally, pleased with themselves and their booty, they left.

(Sister Rosa—Mater Dolorosa. After the war we learned that she died on the first day of the liberation, on the very day the Arrow Cross was finally defeated. When the first wave of Russian soldiers entered the city, they raped all the women they could find. They entered the convent in high spirits, and the young novitiates in Sister Rosa's care were among their first victims. At first, Sister Rosa tried to argue, to protest, to fend them off. Then she just stood in silence, her hands spread out to protect her young charges—exactly as she had stood to protect the Jewish children from the Arrow Cross only a few months before. She was gang raped and killed on the spot in front of the young girls. Then the soldiers proceeded with the girls. Beautiful Maria with the blond braids and fuzzy skin survived, but her beauty and her health were ruined for life. She was the one who would tell Mother the story.)

"Please hurry. The Arrow Cross may be back at any moment. Please go, you *must* go," the nuns keep repeating.

We have no time to gather our things. The nuns have prepared some bags and bundles for us to take. My mother collects whatever she can stuff into her big yellow calfskin handbag. Sandy carries a big dark-brown schoolbag with a handle. I get a matted straw handbag and an umbrella. I get to keep my coat; it's made of fine wool, but it isn't lined for the winter: it's very pretty, though, with its gold and rust checkered pattern. We also collect our caps and gloves. Sandy and I are wearing leather booties, prepared as well as can be for the approaching winter. We are wearing and carrying everything we can call our own.

I don't recall any goodbyes. None of the women who hid in the barn have any illusions about staying together, that they could ever be of use to one another. They are adults. They know that people in groups are conspicuous. Yet I regret having to part from the other women and children. I even regret parting with Mrs. Jonalsky; for me there is security in numbers and in the warmth of others' bodies.

13.

Urged by the nuns to move quickly, we leave by the back door, family by family, trying to be invisible, to let the mercifully dark night swallow us.

The evening is mild. Mother's black silk scarf with the red flower is knotted under her chin and pulled down over her forehead. It won't be light for long time. We should be able to reach our shelter by daybreak. And with God's help it may also rain—Mother could hide under the umbrella.

We're walking briskly along an interminably long road on the outskirts. We need to use the advantage of the darkness; once we're in town, there will be more people. We still aren't wearing the yellow star—what if we're caught? We have to reach our shelter by dawn. Our shelter ... our shelter ... Matthias the store runner, good old reliable Matthias, has long before this been instructed by Grandfather, his boss for twenty years, to take care of us if we ever turn up and ask him for protection. He has been paid handsomely for this and has also been promised a generous reward after the war. He is ready to hide us if we ever appear in his doorway. The address is 5 Heart Street.

"If something happens to me," Mother says, "you keep going on to 5 Heart Street. Knock at Matthias's door, the first apartment on the left on the main floor."

Seeing our stubborn, dejected looks, she adds urgently:

"If something happens to me, you simply must keep going. I may still get there after you—eventually, somehow. You know, by another route ... But you simply *must* keep going."

We don't answer, we don't look at her. We just hold on to her more tightly as she carries her large handbag with all our earthly goods in it. I hang on to my matted straw bag and hold on tight to the furled black umbrella.

"Do you have the umbrella, little one?" Mother asks from time to time, and I reassure myself by squeezing its handle. We've been walking a long time, and the weight of my straw bag is straining my arm so that I have to shift it from one hand to the other. As long as I can reach Mother's coat, it is all right to let go of her hand sometimes, for a few seconds.

We leave the outskirts behind. I keep my head down and stare at the dark, shiny pavement, my feet carrying me mechanically by their own momentum. As we approach the city the lights become more frequent and I sense people clustering at street corners, talking to one another and sometimes staring as the three of us rush past. I don't want to look at them to confirm it, but I can feel their stares now. And some of them must have armbands, military caps, guns on their shoulders. As dawn breaks slowly, I can see and be seen more and more distinctly. Just then, as if to set my heart at peace, I feel the long-awaited drizzle.

"Eva, please hand me the umbrella." Mother reaches down for it without stopping, relieved for the excuse to cover her face.

My hand holds on hard to the umbrella. My left fingers have cramped from squeezing it so hard. Oh what a relief to hand it back to her. She can hide in its shadow, and I can escape the terrible responsibility of being in charge of her shelter.

I lift my left arm to give it back to her, but all I see is the handle. Who can describe the nightmare? I've lost the umbrella! The black, shiny fabric is gone. All I'm holding is the handle and the useless spokes, the skeleton of an umbrella. Mother's life was in my hands, and no matter how hard I squeezed, I've let it slip through my fingers, to her awful destruction. I stare at her in mute horror, unable to whisper an explanation.

Mother looks at my offering and without stopping our march signals to me that it doesn't really matter. She pulls her scarf ever farther down her forehead. We're getting closer and closer to 5 Heart Street.

Heart Street, Heart Street, Heart Street … My heart is pounding, and I'm sure the whole city can hear it. I see something red, soft, heart shaped, and I force myself to think of a red gingerbread heart with red and white icing. Grandfather bought us a gingerbread heart like that last year, when we were at a fair in the mountains. Five Heart Street. Heart, Heart, Heart Street. And Matthias will be glad to see us. Everyone has always been glad to see Sandy and me, whenever we had been taken to the store or to the workshop. "You little sweethearts," they used to say. "So pretty, so well mannered, so well dressed." They will smile when they see us, and we're almost there. No, no, I should *not* think of those people huddled together on the street corners. I should *not* check whether they're wearing the red, white, and green armband of the Arrow Cross, with guns on their shoulders. I walk to avoid the growing sharp shadows they cast over the walls, the jagged, wicked shadows they cast over the pavement. I would like to walk in shadow—I don't want to be seen. But I fear to see the dark bodies that cast the shadow. I won't look either, I won't, I won't. We must be almost there.

It's dawn when we enter the two-storey yellow stucco house. It's still dark inside the damp entrance—a good, kind, embracing darkness. We turn left and approach a glass door covered on the inside by a white chintz curtain. We knock gently, ever so gently. After a moment the door opens.

The Bridge

Recollections: Farewell

Revolving Mirrors—Triple portrait (oil)

Self-Portrait I (watercolour)

Self-Portrait II (watercolour)

Portrait of Ron (watercolour)

Portrait of Rob (watercolour)

Recollections: Separation from Grandfather ("Please don't kiss us goodbye")

Recollections: Away from the Light ("Eva, please hand me the umbrella")

Recollections: Hiding in Daylight (We came to ask for a blanket)

Recollections: Fire and Ice (We are driven)

At the Water's Edge: About to be shot into the Danube

Recollections: Last in the Line (Entering the ghetto)

Budapest—Memories of a City I (oil)

Budapest—Memories of a City II (oil)

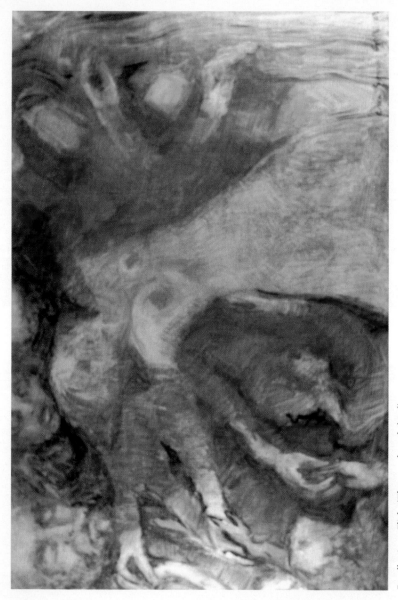

Recollections: Flight (Those we leave behind)

It's Matthias, our saviour, Matthias to whom Grandpa had entrusted our lives. Matthias, protect us, give us shelter and food, take us, hide us. We've made it.

But *this* Matthias, the one who opens the door, is not at all our kind, cordial Matthias. He is reluctant to let us in—he would rather send us away the moment he opens the door a crack and sees us. But he still lets us in. We stand in the narrow anteroom to his small, windowless kitchen. He does not invite us in any farther. I understand perfectly—he let us in this far only to avoid being seen with us, not to save us from being seen.

"You must *go*," he whispers urgently. "I cannot ... I *cannot* ... My wife and me, we're already being watched. The Arrow Cross members in the house know I've been working for a Jew. Mr. Nagy, my next-door neighbour, is a big shot in the party. He already suspects me. He really does, I am not just *saying* ... He keeps an eye on me all the time."

"But we can't go away like this," Mother pleads. "We must ... we need ... *Please*, Matthias ..." I feel that she's shaken.

Matthias cannot be moved. His mind was made up even before he saw us. "Mr. Nagy, he just stands inside his doorway staring at me and singing, 'Where are the snows of yesterday? Everything is coming to an end.' There is nothing I can do—you must leave right away."

Do we get a bite to eat in the doorway? I don't remember. All I do remember is how horrible it is to leave Matthias's curtained hallway and the protection of its shadowy entryway. I also realize that when we get out on the street, we will be in clear, bright daylight.

Stricken by the news, my mother understands that we would be wasting our time to go on begging or arguing with Matthias. He isn't wicked; he's merely afraid. He has a hard look while he's talking to us, but his excuse may be real nonetheless. I shudder at the thought of Mr. Nagy from the Arrow Cross watching him through the white chintz curtains. In my imagination I hear him vividly as he sings his frivolous song, waiting for Matthias, the Jewish hireling, to give himself away. I'm sure Mr. Nagy is lying in wait, asking himself, "Is today the day he admits those stinking Jews into his house? I better keep a close watch."

I see this scene so vividly that I actually don't mind when we leave Matthias's hallway. Anything to get away from the gloating laughter of the imaginary Mr. Nagy and from Matthias's stony face.

Mother will have to sew back on our yellow stars as soon as we find a spot where no one can see us. We would be shot if an Arrow Cross man noticed we had taken them off even for a moment. We take the side streets whenever we can, the boulevard only when we have to. To my surprise, after a while we're back in our own district, the Pest side of the Margaret Bridge where in the summer our house had been declared a Jewish house. But before we reach our street, Mother pulls us quickly into a doorway. 28 Tatra Street, says the number plate. We press ourselves flat against the wall in the deep shadow cast by the doorway. I see a man's silhouette pass. Mother had recognized him as an Arrow Cross patrol. Quickly she draws us into the central courtyard of the six-storey apartment house. "We'll try to stay here," she tells us.

The man she talks to is a tall, lean man with thick glasses. He makes it clear we aren't welcome:

"There are too many people here already. Twice, three times as many as there should be. We can use only a portion of the house, since some of the Christian tenants decided to stay here. During the air raids they're using the bomb shelter; we Jews are supposed to stay in the coal cellar, and it's already too crowded."

Even so, he admits us. He knows and we know there are no alternatives left. We find ourselves in a room in a crowded three-room apartment. There's still some furniture left in the apartment. We are sharing it with several other mothers and children. One of them, the woman closest to our corner, is Ella; she has big, hazel eyes and a mouth that must have smiled easily not so long ago, and she's hugging her little boy to herself. He's sixteen months old and I can hardly wait to play with him.

Mother removes two square cushions from the armchair and puts them on the floor. Sandy and I will share these—see, we already have a bed. We'll use our coats as blankets. I'm quite pleased with the arrangement. If only I could forget about all the strangers in the house and all the Germans and Arrow Cross men outside, it would be like playing house.

Mother has carefully sown back our yellow stars. We're no longer hiding, no longer pretending we can find our own escape, our own shelter. We sleep in the apartment with a crowd of other Jews who are just as trapped; we rush down to the coal cellar with them when the bombing starts. We share their dread of the Arrow Cross, who could burst into the cellar at any moment. We live with the knowledge that we could be herded to the ghetto to be shot or starved or beaten to death, or to the Danube to be shot and dumped into the water. We have accepted that we have no private hopes, private options. We are as helpless as the other Jews around us. We belong.

14.

It's a bright, sunny day in early December. In our light woollen coats, Sandy and I aren't especially cold yet. Each of us squeezes Mother's hand firmly while we walk at a snail's pace—so it seems to me—keeping to the grey walls of the four- and five-storey apartment houses on Tatra Street.

We walk calmly and steadily. Only my fear of reaching our destination makes me wish I could halt at each step, postpone the moment when we reach the corner and have to leave the shelter of the walls to cross the street. On the road there is no protection. I'll be in full view with nowhere to run. Not that running would help if you were in the grip of a soldier's hand, or being shot at—yet you feel you can turn toward the wall, hide, take shelter in a doorway or a shop entrance. Of course, more than for any other reason, I can hold those fears at bay because on the side-walk we're walking in the shadow of Mummy, our walking shelter. Dark haired, dark eyed, in her light green overcoat and with her heavy yellow handbag, she is our live shelter. In the bag she carries all our food and money—everything we can call our own on this earth. Her hand, the mere touch of her coat is my shield, my security against the fear laying in wait to seize me in its icy hands. Again I hear those words I must never think about: *snipped off, taken away* ...

"As long as I can hold you Mummy, I'm all right ..."

But now Mummy stays in the shadow of a big grey house. Sandy and I have to cross the street alone. Some young men are standing on the opposite sidewalk, talking and laughing in the fresh, sunny December air, the way young men do anywhere. Except these ones are wearing the red-white-green armbands of the Arrow Cross and carrying rifles on their shoulders. They look relaxed—would that they never tense up, turn toward us. Sandy and I have a mission: we have to pass them on our way to the apartment house where we used to live, the second house on this narrow little side street. It is *our* house, the home where we used to live. That time seems ages ago. We haven't been there for six weeks. And though the house should become our shelter—I can still picture the familiar smile of Mrs. Szucs, the janitor's wife, who has known Sandy and me since birth—I also know that the house has changed. Last time we had to leave furtively, afraid we would be caught if we stayed. There's no way for us to know what's waiting today beyond the big brown gate or on the marble steps that lead to the landing. I'm staring at the young men I have to pass and praying that I can make it inside.

I feel a film of perspiration on my back as I step down from the curb, and my feet are numb, they can't feel the ground. My steps are rigid, I'm forcing my feet to move. The young men in front of the hardware shop are still chatting among themselves. Maybe they'll let the two of us pass, even though we're wearing the yellow star on our coats. My coat is check-ered with big squares of brown, yellow, and rust—maybe my star isn't standing out clearly. And the paint shop has a bright yellow sign, so that when the young men are blinking at the sun they can't see it between all the gold and yellow. "Let us just pass, just pass, just pass. Almost there, almost ..."

Holding on to Sandy's hand, I enter the wide flight of marble stairs beyond the heavy wooden gate. The gate Grandfather was guarding only a few weeks ago. It is a completely different gate now. It is open, and the people in the house are not the same people. But some things are still there: the janitor's door, and the smell of fried onions. It's hard to tell whether it comes from freshly cooking food or simply the permanent fog left by the innumerable pots of paprika-potato cooked over the years. I have been here before. It's the same, it must be the same house.

Sandy knocks gently on the glass window of the door. Mrs. Szucs answers, and I'm flooded with elation at the sight of her familiar figure. She's an elderly woman with a dark-grey scarf tied under her chin. She wears the same scarf all the time, indoors and out, summer and winter. I try to conjure up her smile. She *will* smile when she sees us again. She had always smiled at us.

But when her face appears behind the chintz curtain, it is pale. As she emerges from her small kitchen into the half-lit hallway, her brow looks like parchment and is wrinkled with an almost imperceptible frown. But the smile *must* be there, I insist to myself. Surely she must be smiling.

She glances around quickly and beckons us into the kitchen. "We've come to ask you for something we can sleep on," Sandy says in a clear, matter-of-fact voice. "You see, we have nothing to sleep on or cover our-selves with."

Mrs. Szucs is not alone in the kitchen. Sitting at the narrow table is old Auntie Susie, the maid servant of Mr. Koch, the tenant from the third-floor apartment. She also has known us since birth, and now she rises with tears in her eyes.

"Wait here a moment, my little sweethearts," she says, touching my shoulder lightly as she climbs the stairs to fetch us something. She's left behind a somewhat reluctant Mrs. Szucs, who also starts searching for something to give us. In a few minutes we are on our way, leaving the house with two pillows and a rough cotton blanket. Old Auntie Susie has also managed to find us a small parcel of food. I join Sandy in saying thank you, rather shyly.

Feeling proud of our acquisitions, and warmed by Auntie Susie's tearful smile, I take a deep breath as I look around the street. The young men are no longer at the street corner. I feel happy to be free to join our mother, who is waiting for us in the doorway across the road. We return to our corner in the room at Tatra Street with our new treasures: we have acquired our own blanket and two pillows.

15.

We settle down in the coal bunker in the cold, grey December. The days are getting extremely short, and of course there's no light where we are. When the air raid alarm sounds, we rush down to the shelter, which is far from our room in the second-floor apartment. In almost total darkness, we descend the tortuous narrow iron stairs to the coal cellar. The air raids are as frequent as ever. Sometimes there are quiet days, and even nights. We always sleep in full readiness for the air raids, but since we no longer have a change of clothes, it doesn't make much difference how we sleep.

I still don't know how, but even here Mummy manages to wash some of our underwear occasionally—we wait for the clothes, hoping they'll have time to dry before the next raid. And of course, it is more difficult than ever here to get into the bathroom. There is one bathroom for the whole apartment, and by now there must be twenty people living here, old men, women, and mothers with young children.

The old-timers look down on the more recent arrivals. One evening Mother manages to warm some water in a huge iron pot over the gas stove in the kitchen. She has scrubbed the bathtub for us, and now she carries the heavy pot, staggering but triumphant. Tonight we're going to have a quick bath in warm water. Mother pours out the steaming water, mixes it with cold water from the tap, and moves aside, towel ready.

Just then Mrs. Schwartz, one of the more snobbish old-timers, actually one of the original tenants of this apartment, enters the bathroom. With the sudden inventiveness of malice, she places her foot, still in its dirty stocking, in our bath water. She laughs in triumph. She has managed to spoil our big event.

There are also squabbles in the kitchen, which so many people have to share. We go out sometimes to comb the empty shops for scraps of food, though of course, the yellow stars we wear mean we're the last ones to get any precious morsels. Yet just before Christmas, Mother manages to buy us a bunch of leeks—a whole bunch. It will be a feast if we can get close enough to gas range in the overcrowded kitchen to make a soup of them.

I miss Judy, my dolly, whom I lost when my parents fled at the last minute from the Gyongyos ghetto and left our belongings behind. Then, when we returned to Budapest, in the fear-heated months of the summer of that year, Mummy managed to find a store with a supply of toys. Wonder of wonders, she bought me another India-rubber doll that was almost the replica of my lost doll.

How I cradled my new dolly: I slept with it, and wrapped her in her own dolly blanket to take down to the bunker at the first wailing of the sirens. Then, one night, grabbing my blanket tightly to my body, I descended to the main floor and from there to the air raid shelter. After the raid, half asleep, I climbed the stairs from the cellar to the main floor, then up two more storeys, with the steady pressure of the other tenants behind me and with the orange-brown doll's blanket still tight against my chest. But when I got back to my own bed, I saw to my horror that the blanket was empty—Dolly, my irreplacable substitute dolly, must have slipped out of the blanket. She must have fallen down the elevator shaft, never to be found again, ever, ever.

Mummy can't buy me a third dolly, but she's guessed something that would make me truly happy. One day by chance she passes a cold, empty-looking bookshop. From that excursion, Sandy and I get third-grade read-ers. *And* coloured pencils. I'm delighted ... my own schoolbook! For over a year now I've yearned deeply to become a schoolgirl, a real first grader. Mother didn't want me to learn to read too early, she didn't want me to be bored when I did enter school, but by now, at five, I've taught myself to read. To be able to read a third-grade reader gives me deep pleasure and satisfaction.

I'm also quite resigned to making cut-out paper dolls with the help of the coloured pencils, a series of dolls that in quick succession take the place of my twice-lost doll, Judy, the one with the valise of real clothes and real little coat hangers. My daydreams still begin with the ritual of listing the long catalogue of Judy's belongings. In the meantime, Mother draws paper dolls for us, and Sandy and I draw, colour, and cut out their clothes. We store the dolls and their clothes in Sandy's leather schoolbag.

Sandy has been quite ill, but by now she's well enough to help draw and cut out clothes for our dolls. And she seems as excited as I am that Christmas is coming. Steven, the blond young priest who has volunteered to live with us in the coal cellar, is planning some kind of celebration. He's the only adult who still has a smile, a kind word for the children. He's preparing a short sermon that he wants to deliver in one of the Jewish apartments in the house. I think of our last Christmas in the year of 1943: we sang carols—Mother has made us love "Silent Night" in particular—and there were Christmas lights, and we had a tree with the Star of David on the top, and there was rich, fragrant food wrapped in foil on the tree, and firecrackers and candles.

16.

It's the 24th of December, 1944. At noon we have the leek soup, which evokes memories of sumptuous peacetime meals of soups with chicken, beef, and all kinds of vegetables. And the memory of the entire family sitting at the dining room table with Grandfather at one end and Father at the other. When I close my eyes I can see that dark-oak table with the white shingled tablecloth. To one side is a polished brown Empire buffet inlaid with a battle scene of Napoleon and his troops. When you look close, you can count the buttons on the tiny soldiers' red-gold uniforms. When I close my eyes I can feel the heavy glow of mahogany furniture mixed with the pink-red pattern of Persian carpets, the lemon and orange highlights on the gilded picture frames. At the table I'm sitting at Tante's left. Sandy is on her right, dangling her feet.

"Alexandra, nicht glocken, meine stumpfe!" Tante's warning is emphatic but good humoured from long repetition. Sandy by now must be dangling her feet every day just for the sake of hearing it. When Sandy and I are by ourselves, we sing Tante's words to the tune of a comic opera, exploding with laughter: *"Alexandra, nicht glocken, meine stumpfe."*

But at the table we're serious and well mannered. Father pours soda water from big green bottles with patent caps and passes it to us in transparent glasses.

It's Christmas 1944 and we're eating leek soup. It brings back to mind all the other soups Mummy has made since the Germans came. A few months ago, in October, Grandfather was allowed to come home from detention camp for the high holidays. The camp, Kistarcsa, was where well-to-do Jews were being held as hostages. (I still don't know exactly what a hostage is. And why would the Germans need Jewish hostages? I'd rather not know the answers to questions like these.) All summer Mother cooked and baked for him, sending him food parcels whenever it was permitted, trying to get them through even when it was not.

She baked meat pies, loaves of bread, and fruitcakes, but what I found most fascinating was that those packages, which Grandfather could receive only by bribing the guards and the go-betweens, were themselves bribes. Mummy baked money into them, and letters, folded into the dough or the meat.

"Why isn't the money burned to a crisp?" I wondered.

Yet Grandfather must have received it, at least some of it, because Mother went on baking late into the night, making up her mysterious parcels all through that long, anxious summer.

Then on the afternoon of Yom Kippur the door opened suddenly and Grandfather entered unannounced. He'd been allowed to come home, a great surprise to us all. He'd been in prison for half a year. When he entered our room, Sandy and I had been in bed with colds. We jumped up and stood on the sofa to kiss and embrace him. In our joy we kept jumping up and down on the sofa as if it was a trampoline.

There were tears in his grey-blue eyes, but he was smiling. And Mummy made mock-chicken soup of vegetable marrow—a strange combination of vegetables that smells and tastes like real soup, with real beef or chicken. We celebrated his return. We lit the candles and prayed. Mother blessed the candles in Hebrew (the blessings were the only Hebrew she knew), and then, in Hungarian, we prayed for the return of better days.

It is Christmas 1944. For lunch in the unheated apartment we have our leek soup, which we share with Ella, the woman who sleeps next to us on the floor with her sixteen-month-old son. In the meantime, Stephen, the young priest with the kind, boyish face has assembled a group of the women and children in a room at the end of the corridor. A few lights are burning. He's talking about love, the power of love overcoming our hunger, the cold of the winter, and the hatred inspired by the war. I'm elated, especially when I see that Mummy has tears in her eyes. She has tender feelings for this kind young man.

Then, after a reluctant start, some of the children join in the singing of Christmas carols. We begin with the most beautiful of them all, "Silent Night, Holy Night."

In the middle of the carol the house begins to tremble and the light goes out. After some anxious moments, we light the candles we keep ready at all times and sing a few more carols. Then we disperse.

17.

At night I wake up to the rumble of an exploding bomb. I have no time to wake up properly. In a split second, Mother's arms pull me to my feet and away from my sleeping place at the window. That place I have just left behind is covered by a shower of glass shards: the explosion has punched out the window.

While I gape at the sight, Mother yanks me away from the middle of the room, and just in time. Suddenly the spot where I've been standing is covered by a cascade of splinters: the crystal chandelier.

It dawns on me that I'd better get out, but I'm so stunned that Mother has to drag me out of the room. We leave just in time to avoid the breaking of the glass door behind us. The room we've just left is now covered in shards and glittering splinters of glass.

Now we're in the dark corridor, groping our way as quickly as we can through the throng, bumping into one another and stumbling over other people's bundles. We work our way down past the Christians' cellar, down the tortuous iron staircase, till we reach the coal cellar permitted for the Jews.

With each explosion a cloud of dust rises from the coal heaps around us. The three of us huddle together. It dawns on me that we'll have to stay here from now on, since we have no apartment to go back to. And although no one says it out loud, it becomes apparent that what we're hearing isn't falling bombs, it's Russian artillery. The Russians are still far away, but they've already surrounded the city. The siege of Budapest has started.

The adults are all certain that the Germans will eventually lose the war. In the meantime, however, they may still kill all the Jews. And every child knows that the Germans have mined the ghetto so that they can blow up every one of us before they leave.

But the ghetto is far away, too. Meanwhile, the rumours focus on a place much nearer. A house on the bank of the Danube a few minutes' walk from the Margaret Bridge, close to the playground where Sandy and I used to play hostage.

"The whole house. Taken out ... In the coldest weather ... The women, the children, the old ... made to undress ... at gunpoint ..."

Mother tries to protect us from hearing the rumours, but it's impossible not to hear. Some of the women and children are crying hysterically.

I'm not hysterical, but I'm trying not to think of what "taken out" means. I don't want to ask where. I see the river, the Danube. But it's usually covered with ice in the winter! And I tell myself we must be several streets away from the Danube. In the cellar, Stephen is walking among the children, comforting them. And next to us is Miss Rose, a Christian woman in her fifties. She lives next to the coal heap on her own full-length mattress, having chosen the coal cellar over the Christian shelter because she thinks it may be safer.

She's the only one who still has food in her apartment, probably lots of it. We often see her eating bread and lard. When she sees Sandy and me swallow hard, trying not to stare at her, she hands us the crust she has cut from her bread. Sometimes there's a smear of lard on the crust.

Once or twice Mother ventures out in the daytime. She tries to find old friends who may still have some food. But she comes home disappointed. She still has a few raw carrots in her handbag, together with two small bags of dried peas and beans. But she is desperate to find something more for us. Because Sandy has been ill; we found out while living with Ella and the others upstairs that Sandy has scarlet fever. At least that was the diagnosis of the frail, middle-aged Jewish doctor who once came to have a look at her. She told Mother the news quietly, angrily, and advised her not to tell anyone. Since it was impossible to get medical help, better not to make the other people turn against us by letting them know what was wrong with her. Quietly but firmly, the doctor told Mother to keep Sandy as warm as possible and to find food for her, especially sweets. Scarlet fever attacks the heart: anything sweet would help Sandy get better. And Mother still had a few aspirins in a little tin in her big yellow bag.

Down in the cellar, Sandy is as quiet and disciplined as before. She shares Mrs. Rose's crusts with me meticulously; the two of us never haggle over food; on the contrary, we insist that the other have the bigger share. Probably that's why Mrs. Rose keeps handing us her crusts. But now we're getting very hungry; it's becoming impossible not to stare at her when she eats.

Then, still during the Christmas holidays, a miracle happens. A beautiful young gentile woman we've never seen before enters the coal cellar with a woven basket on her arm and asks for us. How could she have found us? Has she been checking all the other Jewish cellars in the area? Or perhaps she asked the janitor in our old house, Mrs. Szucs? At any rate, here she is. She is a messenger from Father, who asked her to find us. The messenger of love and food. There's food, all kinds of food, in the basket, and she also brings word from Father. He is hiding in Buda on the other side of the Danube. I don't know what else she tells Mother about Father. All I know is that Father is alive, because he was able to communicate with us. And we hope he must be well himself if he can afford to send us food. The beautiful lady flashes a smile, then leaves the Jewish cellar as quickly as she can.

18.

Another day a group of people descends the black iron stairs of the coal cellar. They're in a rush to enter, groping their way down as quickly as they can. Have they been driven here by someone? One of the newcomers is a woman. Her age is hard to tell because she wears a big white bandage around her head. There's blood on the bandage. I watch, bewildered, as she descends the steps. Will she not topple down those steep metal steps? And how did she get injured? Was it the bombs? Was she escaping from the ghetto? Was she beaten up on the street?

Mother, Sandy, and I sit in the corner of the coal cellar, away from the metal staircase.

A few days after Christmas we overhear that Pater Walter, the dreaded priest who works for the Arrow Cross, visited the Christian cellar of our house. He summoned our young priest, Stephen, and slapped his face for spending so much time among the Jews. He also gave Stephen a warning. As every child knows, there is only one proper punishment for a Jewish hireling: death.

The next time I see Stephen his boyish face is swollen but he is behaving as usual, asking the children questions, trying to give us a sense of hope simply by staying around us. It was Stephen who had led the Christian woman with the basket down the iron staircase to our place next to the coal heap.

That steep metal staircase. Down it the reminders of the outside world enter our lives. Reminders of a world even more horrifying than the darkness, the hunger, and the cold inside our cellar.

19.

One day the fair-haired boy who has been living with his mother in the far left corner of the coal cellar comes back from the outside by himself. As he descends the staircase, his navy-blue ranger's cap with the gold insignia of the Hungarian eagle is still in place over his blond hair.

The boy is ten and thin. His is face is neither pale nor flushed, and his shoulders aren't drooping. He's standing straight in his well-tailored navy-blue overcoat. Ever since we moved down to the cellar at the beginning of the siege ten days ago, I've been staring at the gold buttons of his coat with a six-year-old's awe of shining objects. To a casual observer he would seem quite normal and self-contained, except for the slightly dazed look in his blue-grey eyes and the particularly careful way he searches for words to describe what he's just seen.

"They stopped us while we were walking down the street. One of the Arrow Cross men asked Mother for her papers. She started fumbling for them in her handbag. While we were stopped, she nodded at me slightly to keep going, pretending we didn't belong together. I did. I just kept on going, as if I didn't know her. Till I got to the next corner, I didn't dare to look back. Then, from the corner, I looked back to see her one more time."

He's standing between the rows of rags and mattresses that serve as our beds in the dark, crowded coal cellar. There are mothers and children and a few old people.

"When I looked back from the end of the block, I couldn't see her—they took her away."

He's talking to no one in particular, although several of the mothers, each surrounded by her children, had turned toward him when he descended the winding black metal stairs with the yellow star removed from his lapel.

"I just kept going till I got back here," he finishes the story quietly, meticulously.

I don't remember exactly what happens after he finishes. Only that he isn't crying and that there is a strange stillness in and around him. Probably, someone eventually reaches out to remove his navy-blue ranger's cap with the eagle's insignia, and probably someone places a hand on his shoulder and draws him close. Or perhaps the mothers and the other children just stay frozen, as emotionless as he is—after all, not one of us is safe. What just happened to him could happen to any of us at any moment. We children would have huddled a little closer to our mothers, our mothers' grip becoming barely perceptibly stronger. It may well be that no one at all reaches out to him to offer him the animal comfort of bodily warmth. His loss is perceptible not only in the loneliness he radiates but also in the quite visible way he suddenly grows self-reliant, as if he has just graduated from an extremely demanding school, one we are all training in: the school of survival.

Probably he has to be left alone, untouched, so that his newly acquired strength doesn't snap. So that he doesn't collapse in tears onto one of the other mothers, each of whom is already burdened with the weight of her own children's survival. No, I can't remember anyone reaching out to him after hearing his story.

But then, I can't say I remember anything more. I'm far from an unimpeachable witness at this point. I wrap my arms around my mother's waist and burrow my head into her stomach, into her deep bosom, unable and unwilling to look outside, hiding in the tense warmth of her fragile, alert, vitally protective body. My shelter. She offers it uncritically, unconditionally, to cover up the dreaded images not of the pursuer, the torturer, not even of death, but of the sole unbearable fear, that of being snipped off, separated, broken from the maternal body, tossed into a world left vacuous, airless, and unthinkable. A world without my mother.

20.

But finally the outside world comes for us. When it does, we aren't in the cellar. Sometimes, when there's no shooting, people venture up to the courtyard. Some even have the courage to climb upstairs to see if they can salvage anything from the rubble. I'm in the courtyard when the Arrow Cross men and the police arrive to round us up.

Men, women, children, all of us have to stand in line on the road, ready to be taken away at a few minutes notice.

But where is Sandy? She's disappeared—she must have gone to find a washroom. My heart sinks in terror: What if she isn't ready on time and they want to shoot her? We simply *have* to be ready by the time they tell us to line up.

Mother must have barely had time to assemble her bundle. In one hand she carries her yellow leather bag, over her other shoulder our blanket and pillows. Sandy finally shows up and insists on carrying her own leather schoolbag, which has a handle. And I carry the yellow straw handbag.

We stand in line on Tatra Street. All around me are the people with whom we've been sharing the apartment and later the coal cellar. Yet it's as if each of us were all alone. No one is interested in anyone else—at least, no one is interested in the three of us: a woman carrying a big bundle on her shoulder, with two little girls hanging on to her skirt.

Mother is shifting the bundle on her shoulder: she's worried that Sandy won't be able to keep up with the rest. As usual, I sense her worry before she has a chance to put it into words.

"Officer," she turns pleadingly to the serious but kindly looking policeman accompanying our line. "Won't you please explain to this little girl that she shouldn't carry her heavy handbag?"

But the policeman looks at Sandy quickly and then answers Mother without meeting her eyes.

"Why don't you let the little girl carry whatever she wants to carry with her? You wouldn't want to take this little pleasure away from her, would you?"

To Mother, his words make it sound like we're about to be taken to the Danube. We're being escorted slowly toward St. Stephen Boulevard. Once on it, we'll find out which way the Arrow Cross will make us turn. Right, and we'll be facing the bridge. The river. Left, and they'll be taking us to the ghetto. No one knows which way we are going to turn.

Just before we reach the big Glasner Bakery on the corner—the display windows have been smashed and some are boarded up for the winter—our group is made to halt. The Arrow Cross men shelter themselves under the doorway and wait for the artillery guns to stop. When we're walking, I worry that Sandy or I will fall behind, but it isn't much better when we stop. It's cold standing in the snow. The thin soles of my shoes let in the cold and damp and I feel as if my limbs were freezing. I look at the man in the Arrow Cross uniform standing on the sidewalk next to us. He's wearing a khaki coat and strong boots. His cap is protecting his ears, and his face is wrapped in a strip of khaki tied under his chin. I feel cold and afraid standing in the line, afraid of the bullets. Rifle in hand, our guard watches us with pale, dead eyes.

I understand that nobody must slow down or fall out of step once we get started, and I hold tightly to Mother's skirt. I sense that Sandy may be too weak to keep up. I'm looking at the man guarding us from the doorway, making us wait outside, exposed to the cold wind, to the bullets on the open road. I'm determined to remember his face. I'm taking a mental photograph. I look at him, then shut my eyes, then look at him again. I'm certain I'll never forget his face. This way, when I see him after the war, I'll be able to recognize him and get back at him. I think of my wooden fencing sword in our nursery, the only weapon I've ever held in my hands. I'm painfully determined never to forget his face. But his face is like any other stranger's face. The face of a man with no expression.

The Arrow Cross men at the front of our line make us start walking again. Then, after a few houses, they make us stop again. Now we're at the corner of Tatra Street and the boulevard. A decision has to be made.

The men driving us wait for a while, huddled together in another doorway. They must have decided that driving us toward the bridge might be dangerous for them as well, because now, quite unmistakably, our meandering line is being turned to the left. We're being driven to the ghetto.

21.

It's a cold, windy day and I'm afraid to stumble or slow down as we are being driven along the boulevard. I'm holding on to Mother, trying not to look at the numb, sinister city. The steel streetcar tracks are covered by icy snow. If I'm not careful, my eyes may wander to the once familiar stores with their broken display windows, whose interiors are stacked with corpses. Some of the houses have been gutted by the bombs, only their façades now standing. You can see the insides of once cozy apartments, cross-sections of bathrooms and kitchens, a piano standing on uneven legs as if poised for its flight through the rubble. I try not to raise my eyes. I concentrate on Mother's green woollen coat straight in front of me. Sometimes I can't help noticing the bottom part of the walls right at my eye level, the part pasted over with posters, announcements, and patriotic slogans. I'm especially worried that I'll catch sight of the poster of the little girl with the blue eyes and bleeding hands. If I could, I would close my eyes, but if I did that I wouldn't be able to keep pace with the adults. From Tatra Street to the ghetto is no more than a forty- or fifty-minute walk, but of course, six-year-olds don't have much sense of time. Our march seems endless.

Along the boulevard, past the high, orange apartment house with the billboard advertising Schmoll's Shoe Paste. The glittering letters have lost their luster, although the five-storey house still stands and the billboard is still a landmark in this part of the city, a reminder of the times when people still polished their shoes and went for walks.

At the corner here, under the billboard, an old lady used to stand at a little black stove, all wrapped up in black rags from head to toe. Everything, even her nose, would be wrapped up, except for her eyes and the tips of her fingers. The chestnut vendor. There was a time when families would go for walks and parents would stop to buy their children hot, crisp chestnuts. I don't dare dream about the warm, mellow taste of chestnuts, but I wish I could smell their fragrance again—hot chestnuts at the end of an evening walk. Warmth, food, security, excitement. But now no one is standing at the street corner. The old woman must have gone home; she, too, must be living in her cellar.

On we walk along the boulevard, past the confectionery, which used to have the most beautiful Easter display on earth. An Easter egg made of white candy crystals; and inside the egg, visible through the lacework of crystals, a castle of translucent white candy. The magic of white crystals within crystals within crystals. Dazzling. Now the blind eyes of the shop windows stare at us impersonally, their glass broken, and there is rubble everywhere under the snow.

Along the Boulevard of Emperor Wilhelm, we pass by the Basilica, one of the grandest churches in the city. It stands just across the street from our family store, a grey three-story building that is now hidden from my sight by other people. Where could Grandfather be? Will I ever see him and Father again?

It is cold and windy on the road; it is a queasy, shapeless feeling to be walking in a line.

We are driven along the Boulevard.

A few streets beyond the boulevards are the graceful arches of the Danube bridges—the Lanchid, the suspension bridge, and closer to our old home, the Margaret Bridge. Some of the bridges have been blown up; so I've heard, but I haven't seen. What does a bridge look like when it's been blown up?

The boulevard seems dead except for our line of faceless, frightened people groping their way in the snow. I'm shuffling through the snow among drained, colourless, sightless bundles—women carrying children, carrying bundles, brittle old people carrying smaller bundles; we're shapeless bundles, ambling along, not daring to look around ourselves. Whatever happens, one mustn't fall out of the line.

Is anyone watching this? I don't want to look—I don't dare.

The streetcars have stopped running, there are no vehicles on the road. And a few streets behind the boulevard lies the river, paralyzed as well under its sheet of ice.

But the sheet of ice must be broken in places: I remember the words: "people taken out ... to the river ... made to undress ... completely ... women and children ... the old ..." I don't want to picture the river; I don't want to imagine it any more. The world is grey and white and my cheeks are burning with the cold and the sharp wind. I'm frozen to the marrow; my muscles are moving mechanically. It hurts when it's this cold. And Sandy is very ill. I don't want to think. I don't want to imagine where we're going. Putting one foot in front of the other and then again one foot in front of the other. Left, right, left, right ... Wherever they're taking us, one mustn't fall out of the line. Our march is timeless.

We haven't been told our destination, but finally we're told to stop. A squad of soldiers is lined up facing us, their faces bundled against the cold. They're standing at the entrance to a narrow street. This must be the entrance to the ghetto.

The soldier facing us has just announced that we must give up everything valuable. People will be stripped, and if anything made of gold is found, the offender will be shot on the spot.

Mother quickly takes off her watch, then much more slowly removes the thin gold wedding band from her finger. Sandy and I have no jewellery. We stand quietly, the thin soles of our shoes frozen to the ground. My feet must be frozen, because I can't move my toes no matter how hard I try. We're waiting for the inspection to end. Then we wait in a line, one by one, until the soldiers let us in. They stop someone here and there to examine a bundle or handbag. Since the soldier saw Mother remove her wedding band, she is let go unexamined.

After months of fear and hiding, we are finally in the ghetto.

I find out only later that Mother was able keep our alarm clock in the bottom of her deep yellow handbag, tucked away in its blue paper box. It's a reminder that not long ago we were civilized human beings. Because its hands are phosphorescent, we can tell the time even in the dark. What gives me peculiar pleasure is Mother's audacity. The clock is shiny, golden yellow brass. For a long time, I'm sure it must be solid gold and that we've pulled a fast one on the soldiers.

22.

Except for the surrounding guards—a few Hungarian Army regulars, but mainly Arrow Cross troops, and all of them armed to the teeth—I see nothing extraordinary, nothing that tells me we aren't in the city of my birth, that I am in that mysterious, isolated no man's land: the ghetto. True, the streets are narrow, but this is an older part of Pest with three and four-storey houses. For the rest, the streets are as cold as the rest of the city, as cold as Tatra Street.

The only strange thing I notice about the ghetto is that it's the most crowded place in the city I have ever seen. As we arrive, the street seems to be swarming with children, old people, and women carrying big bundles. Some of the children are wandering by themselves, in search of an adult they can attach themselves to. They're orphans, their mothers have been deported or marched away. What if Mother decides to adopt one of them? I see a girl about Sandy's age with long, dark hair and a grim, adult's face. What if Mother agrees to take her with us? After all, the girl is alone and the three of us are together. I cling to Mother's skirt. As long as I hold on to her, I'm safe and no one can touch me. I'm so privileged. I don't dare look back at the girl with the adult's face.

And of course, I notice that there are many more soldiers here than on the other streets. But why? Should we still fear soldiers? The thing we've been running from for months has finally happened—we've been caught and delivered to the ghetto. So why are there so many soldiers still around us?

Though the streets are swarming, the people aren't generating warmth. We simply have to get in somewhere for shelter, away from the bullets, the bombs, the cold. Now that we've been caught, why do we need to keep hiding from the soldiers? We walk down a narrow street, enter a house, and descend to the cellar. We have to find the person in charge and ask for a corner in the cellar. The man we find looks lean and nervous; he has sharp, hungry features. He's smoking a cigarette. There's an acrid smell of smoke in the cold, musty cellar. Mother's request annoys him.

"Isn't it obvious to you, madam, that there's simply no more room here? Can't you see?"

People are already sleeping all over the place, sitting, lying all over one another.

Mother takes us by the hand, and we move on to the cellar in the next house, but here the man in charge won't even speak to us. Undaunted, Mother takes us back to the first place. The nervous man with the cigarettes still looks angry, but somehow he also seems helpless. He lets us join the others in the dark, crowded cellar.

There are rows and rows of people, sitting, lying, standing. There are some privileged people who lived in this house before it was part of the ghetto and who have managed to bring down their own chairs; some even have armchairs. They are more likely to have warm blankets, warm clothes, scraps of food from their larders. Behind them I see shabby blankets, rags, pieces of mattresses with people sitting or reclining. Along the left-hand wall, on top of some trunks and wooden boxes, I see a pale little boy about my age, and his mother. We settle down right under their high box.

Mother has carried with her a cushion from Tatra Street. Three such cushions would make a sofa. The three of us huddle together on it, covered with our blanket. Just as on Tatra Street, the old-timers here are not at all friendly or comradely. Another mother with children—probably sick children.

"The very image of misery," one of the arm chair royalty tells her neighbour. "Look at that woman with her two brats, aren't they the very image of misery?"

I can't remember how long we stay there. Sandy is sick, and we're all cold. Mother tries to get us food, but even when the bombs aren't falling, people are reluctant to venture out to the streets. The nervous man with the cigarette sometimes goes out for the rest of us. He returns with water to drink, and sometimes a bucket of coffee from the charity kitchen. It's chicory coffee, but sometimes it's still warm. Mother has a little bit of sugar in her big yellow handbag. Each time we get a mug of coffee, she adds a bit of sugar. She lets Sandy sip from it, then she takes a quick sip herself. I willingly take the dregs.

I don't admit it, even to myself, but I have good reason to be generous: the dregs sometimes have precious bits of the sugar. Sifting it through my teeth, I'm amply rewarded for my patience.

23.

Most of the time I daydream or try to sleep on our little settee. By now I'm daydreaming mainly about food. I bake a cherry pie for my dolls, and, of course, offer some to Mother, Father, Grandfather, and Sandy. Then I offer some to Mrs. Epstein, our kindly next-door neighbour. During these reveries I bake carefully, with profound pleasure, slowly cutting the portions and sharing them out to my dolls and my family.

I remember another dream. It isn't a daydream, because it has several levels of depth, as if falling from one layer into another. The overall colour is red, but the red ranges from pale pink to deep scarlet. The background is somehow the painting I had seen before my eyes during the family farewell for Aunt Mimi. We're on a ship, under a translucent pink sky. It's the pink of my celluloid rattle, but also of fire, of burning cities, of a heartbreaking red sunset. I must be on the ship, but in close-up I also see my Aunt Rosie, even though she's standing on the shore. I see her and know she's with her other relatives, my family, waving goodbye. The ship is pulling away. I'm being pulled away from the shore, from my people, those I love and who love me in return. By now I don't see their faces, yet my parents must also be on the shore, because my heart is aching, as if the air is being drained from my lungs. The air is getting thinner and thinner as we're pulling away, pulling away. This is my farewell to all of them, and I know, profoundly, that I will never see this shore or those people again. Figures left behind, waving white kerchiefs. Figures in white, in sheets of white, waving.

There's a large, undefined female figure in the background of the whole scene. My aunt? My mother? The God I pray to every night before I sleep? When I'm pulled away from those figures on the shore, am I abandoning them or am I being abandoned?

I wake to the joyful reassurance that I am in a damp, cold cellar in the ghetto, sitting on a small mattress with my mother and sister. I can touch them, feel them. I am with them.

The daydreams about my doll Judy and her valise are becoming more and more urgent. Armed people enter the cellar. Two Hungarian soldiers: loud, accusatory:

"Are any of you hiding weapons? Do you know anyone who is?"

There's an old man in the corner with a bandaged head who has gone insane. He smiles and then moans, and sometimes screams in anger, cursing someone or something. I can never understand him clearly. Now he moves closer to the soldiers with a broad grin on his face and points in our direction. They approach him cautiously, then look at us with suspicion. The two women in their armchairs are trying to explain to them that the man is not in his right mind. The soldiers make a cursory check of the dark, cramped cellar and leave in disgust.

Another day the door opens and the dark figures of two German soldiers appear in the cellar. My heart skips. They aren't loud, but their words are fast and angry: they too are demanding some information. Though I've been brought up fluent in Hungarian and German, I hate their language. I don't want to hear it—the sentences are like machine-gun fire. I don't respond to it the way I respond to speech.

The bombing goes on and on. One night the little boy on top of the wooden box above us wets his bed. Out of fear? Or was it the cold? There are no bedclothes on his box. I wake up to a pungent smell and a horrible taste: his urine has touched my lips.

24.

Sandy is still unwell. Mother keeps reading to us, sometimes giving Sandy a tiny bit of chocolate from her handbag. I also get some, of course, but I still feel very hungry. Dizzy and lightheaded with hunger.

Before we were driven to the ghetto, Mother had given me a chunk of our chocolate. Hard, unsweetened baking chocolate. I'm to guard it in case someone from the family needs it. Probably she's also thinking that if we get separated, I should have something edible with me.

Now Mother is also ill. She no longer sits with us on our cushion on the floor; she's lying on her back on a wooden box close to the cellar door. She has had diarrhea for a long, long time. A day? Two? Three? I can't count the days. She's become too weak to walk or sit up. I watch her, helpless. Now she summons me with her hand to give her a piece of the precious chocolate. It could stop the diarrhea if she had some food, something solid. Under her black silk kerchief, her broad forehead is damp and pale. There are bruised rings under her eyes, and her mouth has lost its shapely curve. I reach into the bag, search around, then reach into my pocket. But there is no chocolate. I want to see Mother's eyes bright and clearly focused again, her mouth solid and beautiful like before. I want her to get well again. I must find the chocolate, at least some of it.

"I've seen her eat it on the sly," says one of the women, rising from her armchair.

She points in my direction, gloating maliciously. She moves closer to Mother, not to help her but to tell on me. Trying to persuade her that I have betrayed her trust, that I've eaten the chocolate she had entrusted to me. And of course, I must have. Not that I ever wanted to eat it. At least, not the whole thing. Having little, a very little bite every once in a while, yes maybe. But all the time I was telling myself that I was saving the big slab of chocolate for all of us nevertheless. I insist that I must have lost it somehow. How could I? How could I have eaten all of it?

But there is no one to argue with, to explain, to apologize to. Mother is lying in front of me, her pale, lovely brave face distorted by pain. She does not want me to feel guilty, and she refuses to listen to the woman in the armchair. "If it's gone, it's gone," she says. "There's nothing to explain."

There's no washroom in the cellar. When the bombs stop falling and people think it's safe, we go to the dark entryway and try to pass water into empty cans. Sometimes the cans aren't empty. It is horrible that Mother is so ill, and there's no bathroom, just the stinking, horrible entrance with the cans.

After a long, long time—there's no means to count days when we never see the sun—Mother somehow begins to improve. It must be by sheer effort of her will. Finally, the three of us are sitting together again. She's reading to us the story of little Lord Fauntleroy and encouraging Sandy and me to play with our cut-out dolls. I am dreaming again about our nursery, my dolls, their furniture, their clothes.

25.

I overhear some strange, wicked rumours in the cellar:

"The Russians are getting closer. But be careful. Just before the end, the Germans will dress in Russian uniforms to test the people in the cellars. Whoever gives a hearty welcome to these soldiers in disguise will be shot. Then the ghetto will be blown up."

The rumours that the Russians are approaching grow stronger. Then one especially cold day in January, the cellar door swings open and three soldiers in Russian uniforms stand in the doorway. They've arrived! The ghetto is free! We're ready to scream, to yell, to celebrate. But for now all the three glowering soldiers want to know is whether there are any weapons in the cellar. They check the corners, go up to the smelly entrance with the urine in the cans. Then they leave.

We're beginning to stir in our rags. Someone has heard that some-where in the ghetto the Russians are giving out bread to hungry chil-dren. When Sandy tries to stand, her feet hurt so much that she cries out in pain. Yet we stagger to the bakery to stand in line with hundreds and hundreds of other starving people. We're all excited, hysterical with expectation.

"We want bread!" the women cry, lament, shout. "Our children are starving! We need bread, bread, bread!"

The baker appears in the doorway in his white apron. He has a big wooden spatula in his hands with a piece of dough on it. He's already handed out all he's got and there's no more to be had.

"Look! This is all I've got. It isn't even leavened yet." He shows the dough to the angry, starving crowd. We cry out in frustration. Some of the women go on shouting; others beg him to show mercy. Finally, he comes out with a few buns. They're filled with something that reminds me of plum jam. Each of the three of us gets a fresh, fragrant, jam-filled bun. I don't dare believe it. And we're standing on a street, and there are no more Germans, no more soldiers wearing the Arrow Cross armband. It's intoxicating, the smell of fresh food, and freedom.

But Sandy is in tears as we wind our way back to our corner in the cel-lar. Her feet hurt terribly. Mother discovers that over the past three months her feet have grown a full size: she's completely outgrown her booties. And of course, since she was unable to move in those small shoes, her toes must have been frozen in the cold.

Even so, we decide to leave the cellar, to leave the ghetto and its cel-lars full of starved corpses. Before we do, there is rejoicing and celebra-tion. In the cellar there are two other women with daughters my age or Sandy's. One of the girls, Lydia, used to cry hysterically during the bom-bardments. Though we sometimes still hear guns in the distance, we've been liberated. Lydia's mother, Mrs. Vadas, is an attractive woman in a still smart-looking grey coat. The three mothers decide to pool their resources and eat together. It seems that each has something saved for this day. Mrs. Vadas has a small jar with six cocktail wieners in it; Mother offers three carrots from her deep handbag; everyone has a few bites, and every-one has something kind to say.

Then, despite Sandy's aching feet, we leave the ghetto for the boule-vard, the city's main artery. On the boulevard the streetcar tracks are covered with frozen snow. Behind knee-high snowbanks are the windows of cellars and the doors and windows of shops. I don't want to look, I don't want to see. There are piles of frozen, naked bodies, discoloured, bled-out corpses. They're piled up high behind some of these windows. I'm holding on to Mother's coat, and as we pass, she covers my eyes or pulls me next to her:

"Don't look that way, Eva! Don't look now!"

Hanging on to her, I struggle with my matted straw basket; I'm weak with hunger and unused to walking.

We cross the boulevard and come to the arcades of a once fashionable shopping district. The stores there are being looted. People are rushing past with big bundles, grabbing whatever they can. A man in a heavy, fur-trimmed jacket and a dark, unkempt beard with an angry, distracted expression is carrying a huge silver tray under his arm. All around us people are rushing by carrying or dragging dishes, boxes, furs, bolts of cloth.

An elderly woman with a black peasant scarf tied over her head watches the intoxicated mobs carrying their loot. She's standing in a doorway.

"Why don't you grab something, honey?" she tells Mother as we stop to watch the looting.

"All I want is some bread for my children," Mother says sadly, pointing at Sandy and me.

The old woman beckons us, and we follow her to a small, dark apartment opening onto a yard. She takes us into her tiny kitchen. On the range is some food left over from a previous meal. It's still warm. The familiar odour of paprika potato fills the air.

Sandy and I gape at the food with unspeakable fascination. We've been hungry for so long. The last time we had warm food was the leek soup on Christmas day, almost a month ago. The old woman in the black scarf invites us to sit down and finish the warm potatoes. Then she takes out half a loaf of bread—the hard, reassuring crust of brown bread! With a long kitchen knife, holding the loaf tight against her bosom, she cuts a large, round slice of bread for each of us. We can't believe our eyes. It's the first time someone has shown us pity and kindness.

"Would she have helped us while the Germans were still here?" I wonder.

What would have happened if we'd arrived at her door instead of Matthias's? And what will happen to her when her husband returns from wherever he must be? Will he forgive her for giving away the leftovers of the paprika potato?

Mother thanks her, and we shuffle after her silently out of the dark apartment.

26.

There's so much silence about all of this in the years after the war. As if we aren't supposed to remember. And if we remember, we're expected not to talk about it.

How many times did Mother tell us: "When the war's over, we're going to tell all these things to your cousins in South America. You'll see, they'll find it hard to believe any of it could have happened."

But we don't leave for South America after the war. And no one around us wants to hear what actually happened. The Jews who survived all have stories of their own, and the others, the gentiles, simply don't want to be reminded.

Between the cellar in the ghetto and the house on O Street, where we're supposed to go, we see men rushing past us. One man, with a tough, leathery face and a pale little moustache, stops for a moment, looks around quickly, and puts on an armband. We pretend we don't see him. The new armband is red, the armband of the Communist Party. Most of these men are carrying the same guns as a few days ago. But then they were wearing the red, white, and green armband of the Arrow Cross.

I know I still can't go up to anyone for protection. We're walking to O Street, a three-storey house close to our family furniture store and workshops. It's much closer to the ghetto than our own house; even so, it takes a long, long time with many rest stops before we complete the journey. Several of Mother's cousins have apartments on O Street; Grandfather's family had been living there for two generations.

We arrive and look for Mother's cousin, Aunt Agnes, and her twin daughters, Ava and Veronica. But they aren't here.

"They should be back soon," Mother decides hopefully. In the meantime we'll move into their cellar.

Pest has been liberated, but we still hear guns from the direction of the Buda hills across the Danube. In the cellar, we can trace the liberation's progress by the Kovacs's attitude toward us. Mr. Kovacs is a heavy-set middle-aged man who can't quite decide whether to express his disappointment that a few Jews are returning to their homes. When he thinks the Germans might still return, he wants nothing to do with us. When the rumours are that the Russians are winning decisively, he's all smiles and joviality.

Either way, he and Mrs. Kovacs eat well; they have loads of their own supplies and probably some from the larders of the Jewish tenants who once lived here. In the cellar, neatly packed crates and bundles are arranged carefully behind their mattress.

In spite of the guns in the background, some people are already moving upstairs from the cellar, eager to reoccupy their old apartments or to share them with the original tenants. The three of us dare not move. On our way to O Street, Mother stopped with us at an emergency medical station. After the doctor examined Sandy, he told Mother that she had little time to live. Her heart had been fatally weakened by scarlet fever. The doctor made it clear that Sandy must not be moved: the only thing that might help her is plenty of rest and good food, especially food that's high in sugar, any food with a sugar content.

The grey three-storey building that was our family's furniture store is on the other side of O Street. Mother decides to open the store and start selling whatever furniture is left. Most of it has been looted by the Germans.

Mr. Kovacs in his neat navy-blue winter coat is suddenly all smiles and good will. He happens to remember that he has a few jars of jam and preserves in his larder. And by the way, would Mother consider a set of kitchen furniture a fair bargain for three jars of plum preserves for the little girls?

Mother agrees immediately, even though Mr. Kovacs manages to include not only the table and chairs but also a buffet and a hutch with a glass door. I wonder how much the kitchen set would be worth without the hutch. One or two jars of preserves? The furniture weighs so much more than the pitifully small portions of food. Yet the food is incomparably more precious than the heavy, carved pieces of furniture. Food is more valuable than gold. You can't eat gold; you can't eat furniture.

The next day Mr. Kovacs appears in the cellar with a big jar of jam. Sandy gets her first dose of sugar.

After a few days in the cellar, Aunt Agnes returns to her house on O Street with Ava and Veronica. We embrace rather shyly; this side of our family isn't given to emotional displays. The two women decide we should all move upstairs, and they help Sandy slowly along the way. We're going to live in Aunt Agnes's apartment, just as they lived in ours the summer after our house was declared a Jewish house.

27.

February is bitterly cold. The two women wear men's pants, several jackets, and scarves when they leave early in the morning. They're going on expeditions to the suburbs to buy or beg food from old friends, distant relatives, or strangers. Four hungry children are waiting in the cold kitchen of the once comfortable apartment.

One stormy winter day, after a whole day on the outskirts, Mother and Aunt Agnes return with a treasure: a small pot, the size of a small head of cabbage, filled to the brim with noodles. The two women place it on the table carefully. There are four children; before each child gets a portion, we painstakingly count each and every noodle. We've worked out a game where the person who makes the food last longest is the winner. We eat slowly, very slowly, watching one another. It's a solemn game. It takes all our concentration to take the noodles one by one as slowly as possible. Somehow Sandy is always the winner. The rest of the children resent her horrible self-control, as if it signified her control over us.

My cousins also resent the number of jars of jam and preserves on top of the high cupboard in our room. Jars of sweet things for Sandy are accumulating there as Mother sells one set of furniture after another. Sandy's life depends on it. I understand why quite clearly, yet even I can't help looking greedily at the jars.

In my dreams, Mother takes me to Dr. Stein, our old family doctor. "Well, Madam," he says, with his stethoscope hanging around his neck. "I have good news for you. Your older daughter has made a perfect recovery." Then, after a short pause, looking at Mother steadily, he adds: "But alas, it is now your younger daughter who has heart disease. She simply must have sweet things. Lots and lots of them. I particularly recommend plum preserves. Yes, yes, she must have plum preserves if you want to save her life."

In the meantime, Mrs. Rosen, Aunt Agnes's mother-in-law, has found us and moved in. When Mother and Aunt Agnes go on their food expeditions, she stays home with the children. One day, the two young mothers get hold of a big cluster of beets, and Mrs. Rosen cooks them all in a big pot on the wood stove, which we've set up in the middle of what used to be the living room. There's lot of smoke and not much heat, but we're delighted when Mother and Aunt Agnes manage to get hold of some firewood, especially when they also get hold of food to cook. There's no doubt that beets have some sugar content, and besides, we can eat them warm. Beets are sweet; beets are good for you. But after four days of nothing but beets, I'm sick of their very smell. I want to eat anything but beets.

Our mothers keep scavenging food. Their most miraculous find is a cupful of rice hidden in the rubble next to an empty delicatessen. Their triumph is incomparable. It is surpassed only once, when Mother finds five or six half-frozen potatoes in the snow.

Now when I go for walks with my cousins, I search for treasure. One morning, near an old, empty toy store, we find some roughly modelled, painted plaster dolls and animals under the snow. There is magic in digging into the snow and pulling out a toy:

"Look what I found! A little cow! A horse! A doll!" Some of the tiny figures are almost intact. We carry them home triumphantly and keep playing with them until the plaster, softened by staying so long under the snow, crumbles slowly to pieces in our hands.

28.

I enjoy staying upstairs. I'm ready to forget I ever lived in the cellar. It's easy to get used to living in an apartment again, even though we occupy only one of the three rooms and even this one room is cold most of the time. It's hard to find wood or fuel. Mother is trying to sell the furniture from the store: rooms full of heavy, carved furniture are given away for food, fuel, the necessities. Yet we're still cold and hungry.

One day Aunt Rose, Father's sister, arrives at 0 Street. She's been looking for survivors of our family in the cold, benumbed city. She's walked all the way from the ghetto to our house near Margaret Bridge to find out from the janitor, Mr. Szucs, whether we're alive. From him she learned that we're living on O Street. She's thin, and her cheeks are sallow. We embrace, crying.

"Dear Eliza, my dear little ones, Sandy, Eva."

She can hardly believe we survived. And when she hears about Sandy's condition, she's determined to beg or steal some sweet food for her. But a few days later, she returns with tears in her eyes. Her face is pale, her eyes enormous.

"Eliza! He's dead! He's dead!"

Mother's heart stops beating. For a moment she thinks that Auntie Rosie has had news of my Father.

"What? Who? How do you know?"

"Frank, my brother. Dead," Aunt Rosie sobs. "A few weeks before the liberation. Starved to death in the ghetto."

Mother always loved Uncle Frank dearly. Yet her relief is clear. It wasn't my father, only someone else.... Anyone, anyone else at all. We can still hope for Father's return.

Mother gets Uncle Frank's old, heavy shoes. They're stronger than her own, although it hurts to see her in men's shoes. They look so grotesque and ugly on her feet. But for her food expeditions, in that ruthless cold, she needs warm clothes and shoes without holes.

Begging, scavenging, trading furniture for food and fuel—the two women keep us alive. Now we four girls learn we have lice. In the cellar, we'd gone weeks without washing, let alone shampooing our hair. The two mothers set out to find vinegar, gasoline, and hot water. It's horrible to have lice, and horrible to have to get rid of them in the cold, unheated room. We're ashamed that our hair stinks of gasoline, and no one wants to talk about it.

Yet for all the deprivations, we four girls are enjoying one another's company. We go on long, imaginary excursions together, and I'm glad to have children around me all the time. ·

When we're hungry, we're hungry together. When one day the two mothers bring home some horsemeat, we all taste it with the same mixture of appetite and disgust. To our surprise, it isn't much different from beef, though we haven't had meat for so long that we simply may not remember what beef is like. It has a sweetish smell and taste, and I try not to think about the poor fallen horse being hacked at by starving people on the street before we had gotten our piece.

We keep hearing more news of our family and friends. The death toll is rising. The uncles, aunts, and cousins who were deported from the countryside are probably never coming back. But one keeps hoping as long as it's humanly possible.

And we're waiting for Father's return.

29.

It's the thirteenth of February. Almost a month has passed since the ghetto was liberated.

Late in the afternoon, there's a knock on the door of Aunt Agnes's apartment and I go to answer. A dark-haired stranger in a shabby black overcoat is standing in the door. He has a red moustache. I stare for a second and then give a start. Then Mother is ahead of me, rushing into his arms. We haven't seen each other since November. We've heard nothing of each other since early December. Crying and laughing, Sandy, Mother, and I are all over this dark stranger, helping him off with his coat, warming water for his bath, clearing a place at the table so that he can have something to eat. And touching his hand, his arm, every once in a while, to make sure we aren't dreaming.

By the stove, Mrs. Rosen looks on very quietly. She's been expecting her own son, the same age as this dark-haired stranger. Her mouth already has bitter lines rushing down to the chin. Her son had been a frail intellectual, a mathematician, and would never have stood the rigours of this winter, the forced labour. What chance would he have had in a labour battalion, taken out of the country to plant mines on the battlefield and to confront the cruelty of the Hungarian commanding officers? So tight-lipped Mrs. Rosen watches another family's joy tactfully, in silence, in the background, her palms flat on her apron, ready to help if needed, trying not to offend, trying not to cry.

Mother has gotten everything ready for Father. She pours water in a round basin and starts washing his hair. She asks us to leave the room so that she can give him a thorough scrubbing before he is ready to embrace us.

He's been on the run all this time, in hiding. He hasn't slept in a bed or had a bath for four months.

The red moustache is shaved off; he had never worn one in his life, and though his hair and his eyebrows are dark, indeed black, the first moustache he ever grew for some strange reason was not reddish, not auburn, but red. It was his mask, his disguise, while he was hiding in Buda.

The moment Buda was liberated by the Russians, my father decided to cross over to Pest. But with all the Danube bridges blown, what was the safest way to cross? He'd never learned to swim and was no athlete. Yet when he saw several groups of people trying to cross the ice at a certain point along the river, he decided to do the same.

"Quite a few had crossed the ice, but everyone said you must be careful," he told us. "And I had to be *extremely* careful because besides my own weight, I had things to carry."

With some of the other men trying to cross to Pest, he had found an abandoned German truck. It still had supplies: cigarettes, canned food.

"Look." Father pulls out a big can that says "Goulasch" in large red letters. The four children around him suddenly get very excited. The word means meat, real meat. The first provisions brought home by a man, a man back from the war.

But when we open the "Goulasch" tin we find only a diluted, reddish soup. No meat, no potatoes, no noodles. Still, the thin red soup brings back the smell of *gulyas*, the memory of real food, real meat. And as the eight of us sit at the table and mother starts to ladle the watery soup, memories of real family meals come back to all of us.

Father has been walking all day. From his hiding place in the Buda hills to the river, then along the bank with a band of strangers hoping to cross, then onto the ice and up the Pest embankment. Then all the way to our old apartment to ask the janitor if he had news of us.

"That was the most difficult part," he admits, although he does not say why. But he doesn't have to: it was in Mr. Szucs's hands to tell him whether we were alive or not.

"But from there it didn't take long," he finishes with a shy smile. "I never did the distance between our street and O Street that fast in my whole life."

Sandy and I are snuggling on his lap, quietly, almost unable to believe our eyes. Yet somehow we sense that great exuberance of joy would be out of place. Aunt Agnes, Mrs. Rosen, and Ava and Veronica are all being good about it; even so, they must be close to crying. When we heard that knock at the door, they also must have hoped to see a husband, a son, a father.

So we just huddle close to Father and ask him quietly about his escape, where he hid, how he managed to find us.

Then, before we know it, it's bedtime.

"Your father's been on his feet all day. Sandy, Eva. Kiss him good night and go to bed."

We accept our bedtime without a word of objection.

For us the war is over. We are a family again.

30.

Revival.

Tufts of anemic, watery green like the stubble on an adolescent's face— it may become a beard yet. Grass sprouts from among broken bricks and sharp splinters of glass. Pale shoots of grass breaking through the tons and tons of rubble.

"Look, Eva dear, the mystery of life; the will to live." Mother points out a tuft of green among the ruins. "You wouldn't have thought it, would you now, that these few blades of grass are stronger than all the rubble? Still, there it is: it's spring, the grass wants to grow, to live. It knows it's time for renewal."

In March or early April, Mother and I take an unusual trip.

We're going back to the ghetto, back to the Old Jewish quarter of Sip Street and Dob Street, the place we could hardly wait to leave behind a few weeks ago. Mother is determined to find little Judy Werner, the daughter of our former typist-receptionist, Evike. Evike had worked for my father for years before the war. Her husband was killed before December. And now Mother has found out that she was taken to a concentration camp. Evike had a daughter, Judy, one year my junior. If the little girl is alive, Mother wants to adopt her. We go from house to house, trying to describe little Judy.

"Do you remember seeing a six-year-old girl with brown braids?"

But, of course, no one remembers. So many young children have been left motherless. And so many died. There's no way of knowing.

We go home, but Mother keeps making inquiries. After a while, she finds out that little Judy did survive, with her grandmother.

Then, miraculously, Judy's mother also returns. She's one of the very few women to come back from camps. Hitching rides on carriages, or trucks when she could, but most of the time walking, crawling, dragging herself on all fours, she crossed country after country until she finally got home to her little daughter.

After our short, inconclusive trip back to the ghetto in April, Mother has made up her mind to thank God in her own way. The city is slowly coming alive after the siege and the horrible wartime winter. People still have little to eat, and they exchange whatever precious objects they have left for food. They're cutting down sidewalk trees and chopping up the fences for fuel. And at night one still hears "Patrol! Patrol!" whenever a Russian soldier goes on a rampage. But during the day life is getting slowly settled.

Auntie Rosie and her husband, Uncle Laci, visit us every week, just as before. Since the war our serene, elegant Auntie Rosie has somehow turned into a tragic queen. With her beautiful high cheekbones and arched eyebrows over deep brown eyes, she had always looked strikingly distinguished. Now, in her impassive sadness, she has acquired nobility. She's dressed in deep mourning, and her face deflects the light. Her soul is sunk deep into the drama of mourning. One day during one of her Sunday visits, Mother bursts out angrily:

"Don't wear black all the time, do you hear? There are children in the house. Stop your mourning. Stop your mourning! Why can't you try to smile when you're around the children?"

Even then I find Mother's outburst unjust, cruel. Auntie Rosie blanches and her lips start to tremble.

"How can you make someone stop mourning?" I wonder, coming over to embrace her shyly. She stares at me with a vacant, distant look and tries painfully to produce a wan smile. She doesn't answer,

Aunt Rosie

she doesn't argue. However much she resents Mother, she refuses to find a more vital focus for her feelings.

Of course, Mother must have meant the outburst for herself as well. "Stop mourning! Stop mourning!" She was screaming at herself.

She becomes pregnant as a way to thank God for our survival, for bringing back Father, for keeping the four of us alive—our little family. We're not to mourn; the children are not to be reminded of the dead, the losses, the pain and the fear. We're to rejoice.

Stop mourning.

In April 1945, I start school. I'm seven years old, and this is my first year. Mother and Father are elated. The littlest one has become a schoolgirl.

Mother manages to make us school dresses. Sandy and I are dressed the same, just as in the old days. Mother has made us identical dresses out of a pair of old, rose-coloured cotton curtains.

The school year lasts only a few months. The children are neglected, hungry, unfed, poorly clothed. Having taught myself to read and write quite some time before the war, I'm an immediate success in grade one.

"Of course you're a good student now," Sandy tells me with a frown. "But only because the quality of everything has deteriorated so much since the war."

She's quite pleased with herself. It takes her some time to sort things out so clearly. I'm nodding seriously. It would never occur to me to argue with Sandy's wisdom.

When the year-end celebrations come, my parents, especially Mother, are elated. I'm given a long, funny poem to recite. I've never seen on her face anything like the joy when she looks at her children's accomplishments. I'll be given poems every year after that. Not that she will ever praise us easily. Oh, no, that would spoil us. She's very concerned not to spoil us and is actually quite critical of our work. She's more likely to say something like this:

"You've gotten an excellent? Of course, it's very nice. But isn't it natural that you've gotten an excellent? We all know that schools are designed for average children. Clearly neither Sandy nor you is average. So there's nothing to be proud of."

This, together with Sandy's remarks, makes me ponder. Am I an average child who did well because of the general deterioration of everything after the war, or am I a gifted person doing just so-so?

There's a sobering thought in both messages.

Still, I'm excited when I climb up to the stage with my recital about the little mouse who decided to eat only the holes in a big piece of cheese, only to find that, to his surprise, he'd eaten the whole cheese. The audience laughs at the right places. Then, still glowing from my success, suddenly I feel like crying. If only Grandfather could have heard me today; how I wish he could see me as a schoolgirl.

But Mother insists that I have no reason to cry. My parents and my sister are alive. Am I not much better off than so many of my friends? And it's true, of course. There are orphans and half-orphans in my class, who are being looked after by grandparents, uncles and aunts, even strangers. Some of them may have to enter an orphanage soon.

31.

Mother is intent on giving thanks for our survival. She's become pregnant. To bring a new life to the world. It's her way of expressing faith, hope, renewal. First I think that our diet of dried peas and potatoes has made her body grow heavy, and I'm too young to understand that she's only starting to show. When I find out the real reason, I'm delighted. I'm going to have a young brother. Both my parents want to have a boy. His name was going to be Tamas. Tom. Tommy.

Sandy and I are hemming diapers; we're paid ten pennies for each one we make. And we also make bibs: embroidered Walt Disney figures with coloured thread. Though I'm atrocious with needlework, I take my task seriously. Sandy and I are proud of all the necessaries we're making for the new baby. Then one afternoon while we're out walking on Parliament Square, Mother suddenly feels ill.

"Maybe she has to go to the hospital," Sandy tells me, turning pale.

"Oh no, it can't be," I gasp. "How could she think of going now? We aren't prepared for the baby yet. I haven't finished embroidering the bibs."

32.

This time, Mother doesn't have to go to the hospital. But my parents have agreed that to avoid another scare, she'll go before the pains start. In January 1946, a good ten months after the liberation, the streets are still unsafe at night and transportation is totally unpredictable. So one day Mother leaves for the hospital with Father, having said goodbye to us calmly. I learned later, when I was old enough to understand, that the doctor recommended they induce the birth. The labour lasted forty-eight hours, and we almost lost Mother. She was still weak from the war, the shock, the poor diet, and the mourning that she wanted to hide from us. Whatever it was, she was told—and she felt—that she was dying.

"Then," she would tell me later, much later, in another country, "for the last time I said goodbye to your father. I looked up at him standing at my bedside, crying. And I made up my mind not to give up. To come back. To fight."

(How similar, this story, to what she told me thirty-six years later, after her last operation: "I accepted death. I was at peace. All the pain was gone. Then I looked at you two, my children—I remember clearly looking at Sandy at my bedside, she was looking at me intensely, gently cajoling me with her eyes, willing me, pleading with me to come back. So I made up my mind to come back, to fight.")

And fight she did.

The baby is tiny, a forceps delivery. She weighs so much less than either of us at birth. From the beginning everything in the house is focused on getting her to eat. Mother, still weak, sits in her armchair with the baby in her arms, nursing quietly, adamantly, interminably.

It's a girl. No one has a name for a girl, so the family accepts my name for her, Ada. I'm elated, and I'm so proud to have a baby sister. And delighted to have Mother back.

While Mother is in hospital, Aunt Rosie shows signs of a new hold on life. Though still wrapped in deep mourning and the gloom of tragedy, she comes every day to ask about us. And the moment she lays eyes on the tiny, wrinkled newborn, it's as if she's made up her mind to come back from her half-life. The dark, tragic Queen of the Night is slowly casting off her mourning weeds. Her visits become more frequent; she insists on being there for the daily ritual of the baby's bath. Then she asks permission to bathe the baby. Whenever Mother gives her permission, her mask falls away and the waxen limbs drained by her mourning become suffused with the glow of life. She holds the baby deftly but gently, then wraps her in a long, soft terry towel.

"You little duckie, you little package, you ... You're wrapped up in no time—like *this*."

While she's crooning to the little one, she begins to smile at her and then at us. She arrives every day, most of the time with a little treat for the baby, often a treat for us. Her deep sadness, her bitter, empty expression slowly disappears.

33.

The first few weeks after Ada's birth, Mother sits for hours, trying to get her to nurse. But the baby is slow to nurse, and Mother's milk, which was so abundant for Sandy and me, is coming much more slowly this time.

Sandy and I understand that it's our duty to go out every day to try and get her something to drink. Of course, the best thing would be milk. We take two large soda bottles every day. There are several places where we can try to get milk: basement apartments that used to be shops but now are crawling with families. Some of these people somehow have access to milk. They have relatives in the country, or they know someone with influence in the distribution chain. Mother needs milk to be able to nurse our baby sister.

When there's no milk to be had, we come back with soda water. Mother drinks glass after glass.

"It will turn into milk," she says.

But I wish I could bring her something more nourishing than water. Somehow I don't believe that water can turn into milk.

Then one day during our morning outing, Sandy and I decide to take the bottles upstairs and then go out for a walk. That day we have no milk. There's only soda water in the bottles.

Sandy waits downstairs; I'm to go upstairs, put the bottles on the kitchen table, and return to join her. Just then the two of us get the giggles. I mount the white marble staircase with the flesh-coloured marble walls but keep looking back to watch her shaking with laughter. I must have missed a step, because suddenly I'm lying on my stomach with the large bottle broken, and there's blood all around me on the white stairs.

Sandy rushes to help me up the stairs to our apartment.

"Don't cry. Eva," she says seriously. "Don't scare Mother—she's nursing."

But I'm inconsolable.

"Mummy, Mummy ..." I burst through the door, wailing in anguish. "I'm so sorry, I broke the soda water bottle."

So far I haven't seen what's really happened to me, and I'm not yet in great pain. It's only from Mother's reaction that I understand something dreadful has happened. She glances at me, then stands up without a word, takes Ada from her breast, and puts her down decisively. Then, in the same movement, she reaches for a freshly sterilized diaper and ties it tightly around my mouth (in our house each diaper was washed and then boiled in a huge pot for hours and hours and then ironed one by one meticulously). Without even changing her housecoat, she grabs her overcoat and propels me out to the street.

It's late February of 1946. There's still no transportation, no taxis to be had. We're rushing toward an emergency first aid station a fifteen-minute walk from our house.

Eva's younger sister, Ada, at two, twelve, and twenty

Mother doesn't say much, just checks once in a while that my bandage is tight enough and clenches my hand securely. I've cut my mouth in the corner, and the lower lip was hanging down before Mother put on the bandage. Though I'm still not in great pain, it's bleeding profusely. When we get to the first aid station, we find that it's closed. There's nothing to do but go home again.

By then Father has heard what happened and has rushed home. He takes me to a surgeon, an old family friend from his native town. By late afternoon I'm in a hospital on the outskirts, where Doctor Molnar can perform the surgery.

Doctor Molnar's calm, smooth face is hovering over me. His lady assistant whispers:

"Those eyes. Look at those blue eyes!"

I blush with pleasure, but I'm also embarrassed. And somehow, oddly, I'm not really afraid.

"I know you'll be very good, Eva, very, very quiet," says Doctor Molnar with the serious smile of a hypnotist. "I have to work on your lip now—you shouldn't talk or cry. Try not to move it."

But what makes me really calm is that I see Father pacing in the background, his arms clutched behind his back, back and forth, back and forth. His thin lips are squeezed tight, his eyes very bright. He's on the verge of crying. I will *not* make a sound, I tell myself. No matter what. Not a sound.

They make an injection in the corner of my mouth. It hurts a lot. Then I feel the blunt tugging and shoving of the needle: the stitching. Then it's all over.

After waiting for I don't remember how long, we're on the streetcar back to the city, and Father is proud of me. Mother will be proud, too. Even Sandy won't be able to deny it, I was very, very good. A true hero. I didn't utter a sound.

On the streetcar platform, Father pats my head.

"Wait till you get well, my dear. No, don't try to answer now. You'll get all the custards with whipped cream you can eat. As soon as you can remove the bandage. As many as you can eat."

I was lucky. Had I cut my lip a jot more to the side, the glass could have cut a major artery. It was Mother's bandage that saved me. For a long time I'm anxious only about the broken soda water bottle. I can't think about anything else at all.

When everything is over, Doctor Molnar gives Father his word that I'll find myself a husband even if the stitches have to show for a lifetime. And no one ever reproaches me about the broken bottle.

34.

One day, a few months later, Mother returns from her shopping with a box of custards. It isn't my special gift, but she had some money left and stopped by at the confectionery.

"Now, children, I have to tell you something," she announces as she puts the pastry on the table. "At first I had six custards, but I saw some hungry children waiting at the confectionery. They were looking at the shop window, hungry, truly hungry. I know that if you'd been with me you would have agreed that I should give them three of our custards."

Sandy and I are shocked. After all, weren't they our custards?

But then our hearts soften. Mother expects us to be as generous as she is, and we nod our heads with approval. She's made us feel that we participated in her decision, and we're proud of her.

And proud of ourselves.

35.

Tante comes back.

We're living on the third floor, with two storeys between us and the street. She calls our names from the street. She's come to see if we're home, to say hello.

"Sandy, Eva, Hello! Are you home?"

I rush to my parents' bedroom window and lean out to greet her. (Our nursery window has iron bars.) I want to say hello, to talk to her.

Suddenly I realize that I can't speak a word of German, not a word. I've forgotten it completely.

I duck under the window in shame. But I never want to learn German again.

36.

My younger sister is more than twelve months old now; she isn't being nursed anymore. It's a sunny, perfectly ordinary day in early spring when Mother comes home with her face heavily bandaged. There's a bandage around the cheeks, the nose, barely allowing the eyes and the mouth to be seen.

She had decided, without anyone's knowledge in the family, to have a nose operation. Now her nose has been broken; her cheeks and the pouches under her eyes are distorted, covered with painful, horrible bruises. I'll never forget how she looked at that moment: wailing in anguish and then sobbing with anger and resentment. It was unbearable to see her face disfigured first by the bandage and later, once it was removed, by the bruises that lasted for a long time after.

But the operation was successful. She emerged with a strong, straight nose, not marred by the bent. It was definitely no longer a hooked Jewish nose.

Her large, generous mouth and her dreamy yet powerful brown eyes under the full arches of her plucked eyebrows slowly regain control over her face and bring its violated features back into harmony. Looking at her photograph from this period, a casual observer would exclaim:

"This is your Mother? She's beautiful. She looks like a forties movie star!"

Yet the surgeon's hammer has broken something. Mother will later talk about the hammering pain whenever she has sinus trouble, and about her headaches, which become more frequent. Something has been violated.

Somehow I cannot forgive her for putting herself through it, for returning home under the heavy bandages. I feel that she had no right to risk her life like that. Why did she do it? It isn't as if we still have to hide, as if it's still dangerous to be a Jew. Or is it?

The gnawing question.

To be a Jew.

To be known to be a Jew.

37.

How does one learn the fate of those who will never come home again? Some survivors are still returning, and they've seen or heard from someone else what happened to this person or that. Some of these tales—twice, three times removed—we accept immediately at face value. Then there are some we don't want to accept at all, or at least, not fully, not as final.

We find out that Grandmother, Father's mother, was murdered at the beginning of January 1945. Before he joined his labour battalion, Father had managed to place her in a Jewish old people's home. By then she had become unbalanced. It happened when Tibor, her oldest son, Alex, her youngest, and Mimi, her younger daughter, were being taken away from her, when everyone she counted on seemed to be disappearing around her. Already by the summer of 1944, she was having premonitions about Alex. He had been deported from Kosice, possibly killed in a cattle car on his way to camp. She also must have heard or found out about the deportation of her first-born, Uncle Tibor, who had been taken from his in-laws' family estate with his wife, his thirteen-year-old son, and his nineteen-year-old daughter. Father had been away with his labour battalion, and Auntie Mimi, the youngest daughter, had been taken out of the country with a special transport. By the end of the summer of 1944, Grandmother was roaming the streets of our neighbourhood, her deep-seated, light-brown eyes glazed, her speech becoming more and more haphazard.

One day we met her a few blocks from the Jewish house where we were living.

"Where are you going, Mother?" Mother asked her.

"Oh, I was just going over to your place, dear Eliza, to see if you were at home, by any chance."

"But we aren't at home, can't you see, dear? We're trying to do some food shopping; we won't be able to get home much before the curfew."

But the old lady does not see her point.

"Oh, one can never tell for sure, my dear. I'll go to see, maybe you're at home."

Then, without saying goodbye, just waving to us perfunctorily, she walked off in the direction of our apartment house. By the time the Arrow Cross took over and the cruel cold of the wartime winter struck Budapest, she was no longer in her right mind. When the Arrow Cross arrived at the old people's home to slaughter the people there, they apparently found the seventy-year-old woman shrouded in a white bedsheet, standing in the snow-covered garden. Just standing there, waiting for news from her children. They shot her in the back of her head.

Grandfather, Mother's father, was also among those who did not return, and we heard rumours. But those rumours were impossible for us to accept as true. Mother always hoped, vaguely and with less and less reason, that the rumours might yet be wrong, that he might still return. For years, she could not give up hoping for it, in spite of the horrible evidence all around us.

Apparently, when we parted ways on that dark, foggy night on Damjanich Street, Grandfather went to hide in the home of the janitor of the apartment house he owned on Locs Street. After the janitor grew

Leslie's family after the war

worried about being found out as a "Jewish hireling," Grandfather joined a Jewish lawyer, Mr. Sas, in another hiding place. They spent several weeks together, then Mr. Sas decided it was time to move on to yet another hiding place. He feared they had been denounced to the Arrow Cross and were about to be caught. At that point, Grandfather decided not to hide anymore. He told Mr. Sas that he was tired of running. He settled into the apartment and stayed there until the Arrow Cross appeared to march the people to the Danube. Except that Grandfather refused to stand in line, so in his case it never came to the marching. When the young lad with the gun and the Arrow Cross armband shouted at him to get a move on, Grandfather stood up and explained that he had been in the Hungarian Army during the Great War and had fought for his country in the trenches for four years, and that as an old soldier he wasn't going to accept orders from a kid with a gun on his shoulder.

When the Arrow Cross lad started to scream abuse at him, Grandfather wound himself up and with his big, heavy hand slapped the young man on the face.

What happened after that is not hard to imagine. The man who survived to tell Mother the story insisted that all the Arrow Cross men joined in the rare fun. It wasn't often they had the pleasure of punishing an insubordinate Jew. In the end Grandfather was carried out to the river in a blanket. Perhaps he was already dead when they threw him into the Danube.

Though the details of his death were unbearable to imagine, or perhaps because of that, Mother refused to accept his death for years afterward. I remember how she would come into our room from her bedroom in the morning with the memory of her latest dream still vivid on her face.

"I've seen him. I've seen him again ..." she would tell us, unable to keep the dream to herself. "I've seen him as vividly as I see you now. We talked, just as I'm talking to you now. He told me ..."

I remember the vividness of her dreams, and I understood even then, though she never admitted it, her sense of guilt for letting him part with us. Yet her decision had been rational, constructive—it was to save the three of us: she had to think first of her two young children.

I was one of those two children. Yet her shame and regret was something I understood well and was willing to share. Without ever putting it in words, I understood her guilt, which would never be appeased. As a little girl of seven, I remember asking myself what size of sacrifice I would be willing to make if God were to question me how much I wanted to see Grandfather return to us.

"I would give an arm," was a saying I had often heard from adults when they wanted to say how very much they wanted something. What if, by a miracle, God wanted to give us a chance? What if the question came up and God wanted to put me to the test? Would I be expected to give an arm as a sacrifice to get Grandfather home? Which arm, though? As an infant I had been left-handed, but by the age of seven I preferred to draw and write with my right hand. Would I really be able to go through with the sacrifice if it came to the test? The miracle of the second chance one yearns for and fears at the same time.

And then there were the joyful rumours. Someone who had recently returned from the concentration camp remembered having seen Uncle Tibor, Father's oldest brother. The man was certain that Uncle Tibor was alive at the time of the American liberation. Uncle Tibor, therefore, must be on his way home. The rejoicing, the hope, the prayers.

And then, from another survivor, we heard the end of the story. Uncle Tibor had been weakened by disease and starvation; he could not keep up with the rigours of the long journey. He was given food, and he made the mistake of eating greedily. He must have died on the wayside after his first normal portion of food.

None of these relatives received a burial. We've never been able to learn their resting place. Except for the Danube, where my grandfather must be resting with the many other victims of late December and January. Mother could never look at the river with the same eyes again.

38.

Children, however, forget more easily. And even if they don't forget completely, they develop a facility for not recalling memories that cannot be tolerated. I loved the Danube, the graceful bridges that had been rebuilt after the war over the blue-green water, the reflection of the river, of the castle atop the Buda hills, a castle beautiful even in its ruins. (The castle was not rebuilt during the twelve years I lived in Budapest after the war.)

I've resumed walks, and later romantic strolls on the shore of the river that is the burial ground for my grandfather, the river that almost became the burial ground of my mother, my sister, myself. And I also go walking again past the house on Tatra Street—number 28, the sign says—the house from which we were driven when the Arrow Cross still wasn't sure whether to shoot us into the river or take us to the ghetto for a more organized, more orderly death.

The name of Tatra Street has been changed. Now it bears the name of a young man killed by the Nazis for fighting in the Communist Underground. So we're told by the official legends that spring up after the war. But none of those legends add that the young man was Jewish; he's to be remembered as a martyr exclusively to the Communist Party, to the Underground. The heroes who fought the Germans are to be revered, and there's no doubt among anyone that the Germans were victimizers. But the fact that there were Jewish victims, that there was a Holocaust that killed a million Hungarians, is simply never to be discussed in public; it is not to be remembered anywhere, not even on Tatra Street.

It's as if the Party has declared: "Because of the great political changes, it is simply not good form to remember. Please refrain from mourning."

Over the next twelve years, not once do I feel the need to enter the gate at 28 Tatra Street, let alone descend to the cellar. In my mind the grey façade means nothing what it used to; it's just part of my environment. The same with our old apartment near Margaret Bridge when we move back in. It's no longer the same house. The Szucses, our long-time janitors, have left, and the tenants are ready to settle back into a normal, stable, middle-class life. It isn't their fault that with the Russian occupation, middle-class stability has become a dream of the past. The once elegant apartments are housing three or even four families again, not because the building bears the Jewish star, but because there's such a shortage of living space in the city, and besides, the old bourgeoisie must be taught another lesson or two.

Whatever hopes were aroused by the Russian liberation from the Germans, some of the Jewish victims of the Nazi terror are now finding out that they're marked to be victims yet again. Many of my parents' former friends—lawyers, merchants, bankers—are accused of being class enemies. Uncle Joe, a successful export–import agent, has been imprisoned for having connections abroad; Uncle Victor and his wife, Emma, are imprisoned for being "hoarders": they were found to have "hoarded" two kilos of sugar in their larder. (They would be imprisoned for years; Aunt Emma died of cancer soon after their release.) Joe Sego's apartment in Budapest has been confiscated, and with his wife and two young sons he has been exiled to a farm for a year. Paul Gergely's wife and daughter, on the other hand, joined the Communist Party immediately after the liberation, and though they haven't exactly prospered, they've been left unscathed by the wave of arrests and denunciations.

Whatever their new hopes and fears, the former victims are being discouraged from talking about the terror inflicted by the Germans and the Arrow Cross. Our fellow victims want to forget, and the gentiles around us resent being reminded of the persecution of the Jews. So I grow up never being able to tell who had been for us during the war, and who had been against us. Which means that no matter whom I meet, there's always the gnawing question: "What would these people have done on that dark morning in December if instead of turning to Matthias, we had turned up on their doorstep? The kind, smiling mother of my friend, Ellie, would she have let me in? The serious, silent teacher, Janos's father, would he have let me in?"

And what about me? What would I have done? Would I open my door today to three frightened strangers if they appeared suddenly and asked for shelter? Would I endanger the lives of those I love to offer shelter to these strangers?

Those questions haunt me, demanding to be asked again and again. I keep seeing the door that shut in our face on that cold winter morning on Heart Street. Number 5 Heart Street.

THE TUNNEL
1952–1982

Eva's Picture on the Shore of the Danube, Budapest, 1952

Budapest is the city where Eva grew up, where she went to school, the city of her first serious friendship with Edie, the city of her first love for Janos. But she knows there is another, parallel city there, the city where she lived during the years of 1944 and 1945. And below those two cities, there is yet another: the city of her mother's youth, her childhood.

Eva realizes: "I lived in three cities at the same time. And two of them belonged to Mother.

"Have I been always too close to you? Why did you make me feel so close? Why did you allow me to grow so close?"

Death Seizes a Woman, a Lithograph
by Käthe Kollwitz

The first month they arrive in Toronto from Montreal in 1978, Eva takes her two children to the Art Gallery of Ontario. They see a show of the graphic works of Käthe Kollwitz. Judy is going on seven; Robbie is fourteen. They look at the drawings, etchings, and lithographs with growing impatience. There are no colours; everything is dark and gloomy.

Eva stops in her tracks when she sees Kollwitz's famous drawing of a mother covering up her child as Death reaches out for both of them. In the drawn, tormented face of that mother, Eva recognizes the face of Eliza as a young woman in the ghetto of Gyongyos, the ghetto of Budapest. But beyond the face of Eliza, she also sees the faces of the mothers of her friends, the mothers of her generation.

And the child clinging desperately to the mother is clinging to life; she's clinging to the parent who alone can keep her alive, who alone can tear her from the grip of Death. Death is reaching out for the child with strong, skeletal arms: the cattle cars, the forced marches, the death camps, the river. In this child's hands, Eva recognizes her own hands; it is she who is clinging to her mother's bosom, crawling back into her mother's starved, angular body. Every moment she must prevent her child from being born into the world. Because what awaits outside her mother's body is not life; it is death itself.

"How my mother did hold me," Eva remembers. "She never really learned to let go, to relax her grip— and probably, deep down, I never really wanted her to."

Judy is starting to whine:

"Mummy, I am so *tired* ..."

Robbie makes fun of her:

"Mu-u-mmy ... I am sooooo tired ..."

But they make peace soon. They agree they've both had enough of the show:

"Mom, this is *boring*. Besides, we've seen everything. Why can't we go to the CNE instead? And you promised we'll stop somewhere on Yonge Street for ice cream."

After Käthe Kollwitz's lithograph "Death Seizes a Woman"

Is it possible they don't see anything? That they don't recognize who that mother is with the child in her arms? Is it possible that Eva's own children cannot see it? But of course they can't recognize it. And thank God they can't.

Eva's High School Graduation Picture, June 1956

It's only in her mid-teens that Eva recognizes the need to tear herself away. And even then it's hard to do, hard to justify. Yet deep down, Eliza wants Eva to accomplish exactly whatever Eva herself wants.

During the thirties, Eliza's parents felt that a girl mustn't go to art school. During the fifties, Eva's father was still arguing:

"Art school? Ridiculous. Name me one country where an artist can make a living."

But Eva's mother is adamant.

"She wants it. She's good at it. Let her try."

When Eva was born, Leslie was deeply disappointed. All he ever wanted was a son. Yet after the first beautiful baby girl, Sandy, here was another, Eva. And she wasn't even beautiful; she was born with the umbilical cord around her neck.

Leslie's mother, Betty, came to Budapest for the birth; she wanted to be present to receive the boy the whole family wanted. But Leslie greeted his mother with tears in his eyes.

"Mother, a girl. This one's a girl, too."

When, after the war, Eliza and Leslie were expecting their third child, they wanted a boy so much they didn't even have a name for the tiny, underweight baby girl. It was Eva who offered her a name: Ada. She took great pride in her little sister and the name she conferred on her.

Leslie is the most gentle and devoted of fathers. When he dreams about his daughters' future, he wants them all to prosper. The future belongs to technology. He's a successful engineer. In his youth he saw himself the proud father of a son. Now he sees himself as the proud father of three engineers—three lady engineers. So he teaches Sandy and Eva mathematics, physics, and chemistry with passionate determination.

But Eva has other dreams for herself.

Writing. Eliza believes in her writing.

Painting. Eliza's eyes light up when she sees her painting.

Acting. When Eva appears in the annual school play, it seems Eliza is equipped with a built-in praise detector. She can pick up even the faintest, the most distant whisper in the audience, if it's favourable to her daughter's performance.

Without question, Eliza is on Eva's side all along. Just as certainly, Eva is carrying the flag for Eliza, as if she were acting out her mother's own dreams, as if finally they've come to dream each other's dreams.

Yet by her teens Eva is telling herself she has to break away, cut herself off from what drags Eliza down, her problems, her anxieties. She must if she wants to become anything at all.

Eva helps clean the apartment, which is an exceptionally nice one for the times. And she's more than willing to help if only it will spare Eliza from overwork, from all the queuing in front of the butcher, the baker, the grocer, from cooking the old-fashioned, time-consuming traditional dishes, and from her part-time work, which often lasts into the night. Week after week, Eva cleans and polishes the ornate wooden furniture, and she often volunteers to beat the thick, heavy carpets with an old-fashioned beater, to wax and shine the parquet floors by hand, as if cleaning the house were her life's ambition.

"When I grow up, I want to have a place that's simple and spacious, none of these heavy gilded frames that collect so much dust, none of the antique silverware that has to be polished over and over. I want to be free from all this; I don't want to end up a slave like my mother."

Eva resents her mother for letting herself become exhausted by the household, which she sees as her family's nest. Paradoxically, what the daughter comes to resent most is the totality of her mother's dedication. Eliza no longer has any personal friends. Before the war she had enjoyed being the centre of a busy, exciting social life. Now the family sees no one but the same two aunts and uncles week after week. Eliza's former women friends still buy themselves new clothes and meet for chats in the cafés; Eliza sends each of her three daughters to private lessons— gymnastics, languages, music—and makes sure they each get at least one good set of clothes every season. She does housework all day and then, at night, works on Russian translations to help with the expenses. Eva feels there's an enormous price to pay for this total dedication. Impossible to pay. Impossible not to pay.

So by her late teens, Eva has begun to live some of her life in secret. She's become unwilling or unable to share certain things with her mother. Yet under her mother's dark, luminous eyes—which Eva feels are always boring into her—she also senses that she could have absolutely no secrets.

Eliza's and Leslie's Passport Photos, December 1957

Next, Eva places two passport photos in the family album, Father and Mother waiting for their emigration. By the time the pictures were taken,

Eva and Sandy had already fled Hungary. Mother's face is as if under a veil. Her eyes look feverish, her mouth bitter and impatient. Father is his usual self. His temples are turning grey, and, with his bushy eyebrows, deep-set eyes, and square chin, he looks angry and determined.

Around Christmas of 1956, it was Eliza who encouraged Sandy and Eva to leave the country. Her husband had argued against it, even while walking the girls to the train station. To him it made no sense, it was unheard of for two young women to leave their family, to cross the border illegally, to venture into an unknown world by themselves. But when after the girls' escape there was no word from them for ten days, it was Eliza who came down with a fever.

Picture of an Old Neighbour, Sylvia, 1957

About a week after Sandy and Eva's departure, Sylvia, an elderly friend of the family who had set out with the girls, returned. She was seriously ill.

One of six co-tenants in an apartment on the fourth floor, Sylvia was a lonely old woman whom Eliza welcomed into her own family. Sylvia had lost her husband and her two grown daughters in the concentration camp in 1944. She had only two relatives left in the world: her nephew, David, who lived with his widowed mother in Budapest, and her sister in New York. In Communist Hungary, which was sealed off from the rest of the world, Sylvia could only dream about seeing her sister again. When the Hungarian Revolution broke out and refugees began streaming toward the borders, which were left temporarily unguarded, it was Sylvia who tracked down Mr. Bokor, a mysterious middle-aged man from the country, who let it be known to some reliable people that his services as a guide for illegal crossings were available for a flat rate of one thousand forints per person. Sylvia got in touch with him, and by the third week of December an escape route had been worked out for Sylvia, her sister-in-law, and her nephew, David, together with Sandy and Eva and their cousins, Ava and Veronica.

But by the beginning of January Sylvia had returned to Budapest. By then Eliza and Leslie were desperate to hear from anyone who had seen their daughters, yet now they could hardly bear to listen. Sylvia's story reinforced their worst fears.

"As you know, we took the train to Sárvár, a small town close to the Austrian border. All twelve of us were supposed to gather in a little house and wait for Mr. Bokor to contact the man who was to hide us in a freight train that was to cross the border for Austria the same night. It had been all prepared and paid for. But by the time we got to Sárvár, the man we'd counted on had been denounced and arrested. Mr. Bokor rushed out to find another guide for us.

"In an hour he returned with a local farmer who offered to take us, but now there was no talk about trains; he was going to lead us through the fields. They'd been ploughed in the fall, but we couldn't see the furrows, the snow was so deep.

"I was staggering along between two men, the guide and a stranger, each holding me by the arm. The snow-covered fields, with a few bushes here and there, seemed vast, endless. After a few hours, every time I stopped to rest, the bushes on the horizon kept moving in front of my eyes.

"By nightfall I could hardly move at all. Whenever I sat down to catch my breath, I could feel the snow freezing on my skirt and my underwear. At one point Eva knelt down to readjust my garters, because they'd slipped down and I was losing my stockings. She had to break a layer of ice all around the garter before she could fit it back on my stocking. Then Eva herself couldn't walk any more and some people tried to help her along. Then I lost sight of everyone else.

"The last thing I remember is that we were getting very thirsty, and some people started to eat the snow. But snow doesn't quench your thirst at all. And then all I can remember is that I couldn't take another step ...

"I was lucky I wasn't left there in the snow; the guide half-dragged, half-carried me to a cottage at the end of the village, and he just left me there to the mercy of the people inside."

But Eva remembers something else about Sylvia's story. When the refugees arrived at Sárvár, they had all crowded into a small room to await nervously for news about the train. There, David's mother—a thin, high-strung woman in her forties—suggested that everyone take two tranquil-lizers.

"We have a stressful time ahead," she told them. "In less than an hour two of these pills will make you feel calm and at ease."

Ava, Veronica, and Sandy accepted the offer. So did Eva. An hour later, while they were staggering through the snow, she suddenly felt so weak that she almost passed out.

"You will freeze to death if you don't keep moving," Sandy told her, pulling Eva up each time she wanted to lie down in the snow. Then a young man, a stranger, stepped forward from the end of the line. He grabbed Eva's heavy handbag and began dragging her along by the arm. At first Eva moved like an automaton, lifting one numb foot after another, but eventually she fell into step with him.

The fields were turning greyer and greyer. The only solid objects Eva could make out were some distant bushes on the horizon. After some

Escape from Hungary, 1956

time those bushes began to move along with the people staggering through the snow. Then it suddenly looked as if the distant bushes were starting to move faster. Unmistakably, they were getting closer and closer. At first Eva didn't trust her eyes, but then the others saw the same thing. By then the bushes were clearly no longer bushes—they were people. A long, dark chain of people holding hands.

And Sylvia was right. By the third hour they were all so thirsty they'd started eating the snow. Their guide had a bottle of strong, homemade plum brandy in his coat pocket and began passing it around. By this time Eva was resolved not to touch anything. David, though, was unable to resist—he was exhausted and desperately thirsty, and he took several slugs. But he wasn't used to strong drink, and it made him lie down in the snow, unable to continue. His mother tried in vain to pull him up. Finally, in desperation, she sat down in the snow next to him, determined to wake him, not to let him freeze to death in the fields. That's when the bushes in the distance started to move. As the bushes turned into a chain of figures moving faster and faster, the people around Eva all started to run. David and his mother were left behind to their fate.

The people around Eva were running as fast as they could. So was she, all out of breath, still being half-carried by the young man. Then, after a few breathless moments, the group slowed down. There was no use running anymore—they had been overtaken.

Cornered, frightened, panting for breath, they watched their pursuers. To their infinite relief, it soon became clear that these people weren't soldiers or border guards. They were refugees just like themselves, with knapsacks and suitcases, and they were out of breath, too. They had got lost in the fields without a guide and were glad to have spotted another group in the snow. The two groups joined up and went on together.

By the time they neared the Austrian border, they'd been walking for eight hours through the snow. By this point Sandy was unable to go on. With her skirt, pants, and even her coat turned to ice, she sat down, insisting that she had walked enough. Now it was Eva's turn to pull—she started pulling Sandy to her feet every time she tried to sit down, reminding her she would freeze to death if she stopped.

"Downhill, *there*, that's already Austria," their guide pointed, taking out his plum brandy for the last time. People laughed and cried and kissed each other. The young man next to Eva embraced her warmly, and she embraced him back. Twenty minutes later they were in the refugee camp, revived by mugs of hot cocoa and a strange, orange-coloured Canadian cheese that was spread thickly on slices of white bread.

Exhausted, they barely had the energy to answer the questions of the camp authorities, who had to fill out forms for each newcomer. Within a few minutes all the refugees were fast asleep on the straw that had been spread for them in the barn. It was only when she woke at dawn, that Eva learned that David and his mother hadn't frozen to death after all; they had been found by another refugee group and dragged into the camp as well.

In the morning, when the buses arrived to take them to Vienna, Eva and the young stranger said goodbye. He was going to Australia, where he had friends; she wasn't sure where she would end up, but definitely it was not Australia. They embraced; they exchanged pictures; they climbed onto different buses.

They never heard from each other again.

After Sylvia returns to Budapest, Eliza gets well enough to take care of the exhausted old woman. She moves her onto the living room sofa and starts nursing her. It does Eliza good to have a daily routine; meanwhile, she and Leslie wait, consumed with anxiety, for news of their two older daughters. Have they been caught by the authorities? Some young people, they've heard, were caught on their way to the border and beaten before being returned to Budapest. Could the girls have gotten ill, like what happened to Sylvia? Could they have been shot during a border skirmish?

The telephone lines in the Austrian villages along the Hungarian border are overwhelmed; thousands and thousands of refugees are arriving every day. It is more than ten days before Sandy and Eva are able to let their parents know they've crossed the border safely and are in a refugee camp in Vienna.

They spend a few months in the camp in Vienna. Eva gets a scholarship to attend the Academy of Fine Arts on Schillerplatz. How she wishes she could stay in Vienna—but it's still

Vienna

not safe, it's still too close to Budapest and to the Soviet Bloc. Also, from here it would be impossible to bring out the family anytime soon. For a quicker, safer reunion with the family left behind, Eva and Sandy will have to travel farther.

Picture of Sandy and Eva in Heavy Overcoats, Montreal, 1957

After a few months in Vienna, the chance comes for Eva and Sandy's university group to emigrate to Canada. Montreal, till now an anonymous pink-red spot on a map, suddenly springs to life for the family left overseas. Now it's a place of high drama, seething with battles for survival and hopes of reunion.

Sandy is twenty-one, Eva not quite nineteen, when they arrive at Montreal. In less than a year they will have worked and saved enough to pay the airfare for their mother, father, and younger sister and to rent and furnish an apartment for all. But the year has been full of fears and uncertainties. At one point, to pressure young refugees to return to Hungary, the Hungarian government threatens to punish their parents. And parents whose children send them passports and other documents are threatened with arrest for trying to contact relatives abroad.

"Please write every day," write Sandy and Eva, but they don't dare mention the rumours circulating about political conditions in Budapest. The most persistent rumour is that all letters are being censored.

"Please write every day," writes Eliza. "We want to know everything that happens in your lives!"

It gets to the point where Eliza can tell from the postman's face whether she's received a letter from overseas: he has a great big smile when he has one to give her. And he seems genuinely upset when he doesn't.

And Eva writes every single day, although there are days when she decides not to send the letter she wrote. On days when she would have bad news, she simply writes a note about the food at the cafeteria, or about the colour of the strange plastic winter boots people wear in Montreal. The following letter, for example, was not sent home, although it included a line drawing she made for her parents.

Today was the twelfth day of our arrival on this continent, but I still feel under the shock of this bitter, unbelievably cutting winter weather in late February. From our window in the YWCA we can see a huge white milk bottle on top of a red brick house, as if the advertisement itself were permanently refrigerated for the long months of winter.

This morning, together with our cousins, Sandy and I were rushing down Dorchester Avenue with its two skyscrapers—the two tallest landmarks in Montreal. In our light winter coats we felt the need to run for shelter several times before we found the address we were looking for. But where could we find shelter in this frigid, foreign city? All the gates of the houses were locked as we ran to the Immigration Office, a twenty-minute walk made unbearably long in this cutting, sub-zero temperature.

During the long wait in the corridor, we had time to thaw our frozen hands and feet. Then we burst into the office of the immigration officer, eager to explain our situation:

Montreal from the window of the YMCA

"You see, sir, we'd like to bring over our parents. They may be in danger because we escaped, we left the country illegally. We'd like to settle in Canada permanently and apply for citizenship right away. We'd like to apply for our parents' papers at the same time."

But at this point the serious-looking officer behind the desk made a remark that dashed all our hopes. We had come to Canada because it was the only country in the West that allowed new immigrants to apply for their families' papers right on arrival. But now the officer said something about the law having been changed. Only Canadian citizens had the right to bring in their families from other countries.

And when would we become citizens?

"Normally it takes five years ... Unless a woman marries a Canadian citizen."

Rushing out of the Immigration Office, it was not only the icy wind along Dorchester Street that brought tears to our eyes.

"There's no reason to give up hope," I kept telling Sandy as we pulled up our collars and tried to cover our faces with our light scarves.

Today was my nineteenth birthday. And wasn't there a young man at the University's Hillel Club who offered to give me a ride whenever we had to start looking for our own apartments? Let's see, what was his name?

I made up my mind then and there.

"Very simple. I'm going to marry what's-his-name. True, he looks dull, and even worse, he's shorter than me, but should either of those things stop me from marrying him as long as he's a Canadian citizen? It could shorten the years of waiting for our family."

But while I was contemplating the pros and cons of bartering myself to a total stranger, I was compelled to return to the here and now, to confront a far more urgent question.

We were too late for the lunch provided to the refugee students in the jail on St. Antoine Street. How delicious that hot soup and warm meal sounded now that we'd missed it. By the time we got to the prison building along the icy sidewalks, the doors were closed. Behind those doors we would stand in line, after the prisoners' meal was over, to mingle with our fellow refugees. The austere-looking prison and the wolf whistles of some of our compatriots made lunch hour unpleasant, but it was better than no lunch at all. And a restaurant was simply out of question. Our weekly pocket money of two dollars was more than spoken for by the expenses of stamps, envelopes, and occasional bus fares.

But how to warm up? The only thing to do was walk toward St. Catherine Street toward the Eaton or Simpson department stores. But on the way we noticed a little shop with the intriguing sign "Nut Hut," and when its door was thrown open by a departing customer, we were hit by the tantalizing smell of freshly roasted peanuts.

Montreal winter

Sandy, Ava, and Veronica decided quickly. "You wait here, Eva, we'll be right back." Then they pooled all their money and disappeared through the door.

They came out with a neat paper bag containing half a pound of glazed peanuts. Today was my nineteenth birthday. The nuts were my birthday gift—food, the most loving and sacrificial gift of all.

The birthday gift also served as our lunch today. Huddling together at the Simpson's entrance, the four of us were sampling each glazed nut with the same loving care and attention we had sampled the noodles our mothers managed to get for us right after the war, twelve long years ago. Huddled together with our cheeks still frozen by the cold wind, we ate the peanuts slowly, in awe of their warmth, their nourishment, their sweetness.

Picture of Sandy and Eva in Front of the Rooming House on Hutchison Street, 1957

All the girls in the Hungarian student group have been given a bed at the YWCA and have been provided meals, sometimes at the Y, sometimes at Royal Victoria College, sometimes at the jail on St. Antoine Street. By mid-May the English courses offered to the foreign students at the Petofi House on McTavish Street have ended. The students are told that it's up to them to find jobs. Even Canadian students have to do this for themselves.

Now the job search begins. But it takes the four girls time to understand the ritual. To begin with, wherever they apply, they're asked whether they have experience. What is someone like Eva to do? Except for a three-week summer job in a graphic studio in Budapest, she has never worked. Now, when she's attending an interview for an office job, the interviewer always asks:

"Do you have experience in this field?"

"Of course," she always answers enthusiastically. But it's precisely her enthusiasm that gives her away.

After weeks of unsuccessful job hunting, Eva gets an appointment at Bell Canada. They're hiring office help. Sandy and several of their friends have already found work there.

"And what kind of salary do you have in mind?" asks the interviewer.

"I've heard you usually offer a hundred and fifty a month. But I would appreciate a little bit more. You'll find me a very hard worker, and it's really very important for me to save money this summer. I'm working on getting my parents out of Hungary, and every penny counts."

The man behind the desk rises politely.

"Thank you very much. We'll be in touch."

He smiles at Eva and offers her his hand. Eva is pleased by his kind, polite response. Of course she doesn't get the job. She has committed two unpardonable sins: she has talked about money and about her personal problems.

After a frustrating day looking for work, in her daily letters Eva entertains her mother with anecdotes about the immigrant experience. One day, one of her friends was standing at the counter of a cafeteria.

"Please, miss, what's the name of that red dessert at the front?"

"It's called jello."

"And the one behind it?"

"Apple pie with ice cream."

"And the one next to it?"

"Black Forest cake—a chocolate cake. Which would you like?"

"All of them, please."

It's only when the glutton gets to the cashier that she's made to understand, ever so politely, that the meal ticket entitles her to one item each among the many possible appetizers, meat dishes, and desserts. The Canadian students in the cafeteria at Royal Victoria College are extremely careful of their figures; they stare at these unabashedly gluttonous Central European girls as if they're a foreign species.

It takes several weeks for Eva to learn the etiquette of job hunting. Then she finds a well-paid job as a filing clerk for the Canadian Pacific Railway. As the dark days of frustration disappear, she writes to her parents about the chances for evening art courses, and for scholarships, and about the steps they will have to take to reunite. By the beginning of summer, both Sandy and Eva have steady work and are renting a room for six dollars a week in a rooming house on Hutchison Street. Each is following an unwritten law not to spend more than a dollar a day for food. They will save the rest of their earnings for the family.

They also take on extra jobs. They babysit on the weekends, and Eva has a part-time job for Saturday and a few evenings a week as an assistant to the owner of an art studio on Sherbrooke Street. She is also taking evening courses at the university. The two sisters are a team, working together, saving together, preparing the ground for the family reunion.

One day, walking home from work, Eva's eye is caught by a blouse at Woolworth's. It's on sale for ninety-nine cents. She swallows hard. She's nineteen years old and all her clothes are hand-me-downs, charity pieces.

This is her first real purchase: a crisp cotton blouse with red, blue, and white stripes—colourful, youthful, attractive.

She goes home to show her purchase triumphantly. "Look, Sandy, I bought myself a blouse for less than a dollar."

Sandy is busy in the basement kitchen, which is shared by all the other tenants of the rooming house. She's standing in front of the stove, preparing dinner for her fiancée, Ernie, and she isn't sure how to sauté the chicken without burning the bread crumbs. She glances at Eva matter-of-factly:

"Well, it's your business, if you don't feel like saving for the family."

Hurt to the quick, even so Eva decides to act ladylike and refrains from retaliating. No, she certainly will not point out the obvious, that Sandy spends far too much of her hard-earned money cooking elaborate meals for her fiancée. No, no, Eva simply will not stoop so low as to point that out—today. (It so happens she pointed it out yesterday, and the day before that.)

Eva retreats to her small room in the basement, wounded into silence. Every penny counts, and she feels almost physical pain whenever she has to spend a penny more than what she's allotted herself for room and board. She has come to view herself as a machine: her only purpose is to earn and to save. And every dollar, every cent becomes a test, a measure of stamina—a measure of love.

Picture of Sandy and Eva's First Apartment

Of course, she knows that Sandy is also anxious about all the hoops they have to jump before they can achieve their goal.

"You have to prove that you have a steady job."

"You have to have five hundred dollars in the bank to be able to sponsor them, to show you can support them for a while on your own."

"You have to be able to pay for their transportation overseas."

Sandy and Eva jump through all the hoops.

Up to the very last minute, no one knows whether Mother, Father, and Ada will be allowed to leave Hungary. Will the family ever see one another again?

Then, on New Year's Day, the telephone rings.

Eva and Sandy are sitting in the master bedroom, sewing bedspreads and covers for all the second-hand furniture they've just bought and moved into their small two-bedroom apartment.

They sew by hand. There are miles and miles of frills to be sewn to go all around the bedspread, the covers for the chairs and night tables.

"Hello? You have a telegram," the operator announces.

Sandy and Eva stick their ears to the same receiver. Waiting for the message, each listens with her whole body, her whole being.

The operator reads the telegram over the phone:

"We are in Amsterdam. Arriving Montreal tomorrow."

Sandy and Eva don't look at each other. Then each covers her face with her hands. Their sobs come from the same depth. Both sisters are weeping. Side by side, yet each by herself. Weeping with joy.

Since her early teens, Eva's favourite novel has been Thomas Mann's *Joseph and His Brothers*. It was in Montreal that she found the fourth volume of the tetralogy: *Joseph the Provider*. The book ends with the arrival into Egypt of Jacob and his tribe with camels and donkeys laden with all their earthly goods. Having left everything else behind, they arrive into the welcoming arms of Joseph. After years of anxiety, grief, and mourning, parent and child are able to reunite. Now, Eva is reliving the reunion of Jacob and Joseph while sewing interminable lines of cotton frills, which she is certain by now could wind around the globe. And when she arrives at the point where the patriarch is helped from his camel and walks blindly into the open arms of his child, Joseph, she is shaking too hard with sobs to keep silent. Then she notices that through the thick double layer of the horrible blue fabric, she has been stitching the frills to her own skirt and must start over again.

That night Sandy and Eva don't go to bed at all. By dawn every surface in the cramped little apartment has been covered with the light-blue cotton fabric. And there are frills, frills, frills around the spreads, the covers, the curtains, as if the frills could hide the clumsy, worn-out furniture and the ugly living room: three walls painted strawberry pink, the fourth one spinach green. Then, at daybreak, they take a hot bath and order a taxi. It's still dark when they arrive at Dorval Airport.

Picture of Eliza, Leslie, and Ada in Heavy Overcoats, January 1958

Sandy, Eva, and Ernie are waiting for the family in the overheated wooden shack that is the arrivals area. Outside it is twenty below—a normal January day in Montreal.

The plane is on its way.

The plane is almost here.

The plane has just arrived.

Eva bites her hand so hard that it shows the marks for days. Not to cry out in impatience. Not to cry out in joy.

They see three heavily clad immigrants, a man, a woman, and a child, descend from the plane. Father, Mother, and Ada. Among the well-dressed Western travellers from Amsterdam, they look like an etching of nineteenth-century Eastern European immigrants. Father wears a long fur-lined overcoat and an old-fashioned dark hat; Mother a heavy, thick-lined grey coat and a burgundy turban. The little girl is also bundled up against the cold in a way that looks out of place.

Then they appear at the door.

For a moment there are no words, only the mad rush of kissing, crying, falling into one another's arms—the bodies of the three children and two parents form a heaving tangle, like willows swaying together in a storm. Then they tear themselves away to stare at one another and assess the changes.

So much has happened in a year.

Father, Mother and Ada. Their clothes are so unlike what they would wear in Hungary. Yet they are also a striking contrast to what people would wear in Montreal. Clearly, they want to break with everything they have ever been used to, as if to demonstrate their willingness to reshape themselves in their own outlandish image of the New World. The tribe of Jacob, arriving with camels and donkeys laden with all their earthly goods.

Mother is forty-four that year, Father in his late fifties, little Ada only twelve. They have been allowed to bring three beat-up suitcases, which were carefully checked at Budapest Airport to make sure they contained no valuables. And Eliza is carrying a huge, shapeless old handbag on her arm, an oversized shabby old thing she would not allow to be stowed as cargo.

Family Picture in the Living Room on Randall Street, 1958

Eva and Sandy's parents are bright, vital, energetic people. They have given up everything to be with their children. They are ready to start all over. Not to look back, not to regret, not to mourn. To turn toward the future.

The cab back to Montreal carries them past snow-covered fields. Abandoned shacks dot the roadsides, with rows of small, boxlike houses in the distance. Patches of their tawdry metal roofs peek through the snow.

"Beautiful, beautiful, this is the most beautiful country," Father beams. He can hardly wait to start looking for a job tomorrow. His English has been honed and polished to perfection over the past year. He has brought along his books, the articles he has published, descriptions of his inventions. He will start life again at fifty-six and begin looking after his family again, just as before. He refuses to look back at all.

The six of them crowded into the taxi can still hardly believe their eyes. Eva and Sandy embrace their mother, they embrace their father. Ada in the middle of them all feels suddenly left out. She starts to cry. Her two sisters embrace her too, laughing:

"Don't cry, Ada—you'll be delighted when we get home. We bought you the toys you've always wanted. Dishes for your dolls, equipment for a little store, even a tiny cash register that works. And lots and lots of stationery. Wait till we get home."

But Mother is taken aback by the shacks, by the snow, by the grey uniformity of the street where they live. Randall Street. Sandy's and Eva's letters had described the luxury, the comfort, of a North American city. But those boxes—do all houses in Canada look like boxes? But when they enter the apartment with the ugly oil stove standing in the middle of the hallway, suddenly all are deeply touched. The family's new home—the hearth—Sandy and Eva's accomplishment.

"And here is your bedroom." Sandy and Eva point to the small master bedroom, which they've just furnished second-hand.

Everything is clean, and covered with cotton spreads and tablecloths of the same light-blue pattern. But when Mother places her heavy handbag on the night table, the table collapses. Under the cotton frills, it's made of cardboard. In fact, it's a grocery carton from Steinberg's.

Now before sitting down on the bed, Mother carefully lifts the cotton frills.

"Just to make sure *this* isn't cardboard."

They all laugh and cry, embracing each other over and over again.

The family sits together in the living room, which also serves as Eva and Ada's bedroom. Mother opens her suitcases packed with clothes for themselves, some bed linen almost totally useless—the shape and size of blankets and pillows are quite different in Montreal from those in the old country—and two silver candlesticks, the only mementoes from the old home. Then Mother unpacks the gifts for Sandy and Eva. She has brought them coats, blouses, dresses, all made from the newest materials available, the most costly and therefore the most fashionable in Budapest: nylon—something that's just gone out of fashion on this continent.

She has also brought warm winter coats for each member of the family, and a fur coat. It will probably fit Eva. The only thing Europeans know about Montreal is that the winters are bitterly cold. The sheepskin fur coat is heavy and stiff; it could stand by itself, like a tent, in the middle of the bare-floored living room.

Then finally, from the third suitcase, Eliza pulls out a rolled-up canvas: an oil portrait of Ethel, Eliza's mother, the three girls' grandmother. Eva offers to have it stretched soon. It will go over the double bed in the master bedroom.

Only now does it occur to Eva to ask about the handbag.

"Mother, what's in that? Can we see?"

Eva carries the enormous handbag from the bedroom and opens it. It's packed with family photos, papers, postcards, and the three sisters' childhood drawings and poems prepared for long-ago birthdays, anniversaries. The record of the home that was, the family that was.

"We'll look at all this later," says Eliza, carefully closing the rusty zipper that refuses to run smooth.

In that old, shapeless bag is the family history. The family she had left behind in the cemeteries of Budapest, in the silt of the Danube, in the mass graves of Eastern Europe.

That huge, misshapen old handbag is the ship in which the family has crossed to the New World.

Photos of Weddings and Graduations, Montreal, 1958–1964

After the first few weeks of joy, Mother shows the curious symptoms of a long-distance swimmer who after a long and dangerous stretch beyond her endurance feels that she can collapse safely. Father finds a job as a research chemist and is more absorbed in his work than ever. Sandy and Ernie, recently married, want to move out and get their own apartment as soon as possible. Ada is in grade six, doing extremely well in picking up the language and making headway in her subjects—she isn't at home during the day either.

Eva works in an office in the daytime and takes evening courses in Fine Arts and Literature at Sir George Williams University toward her B.A. To be able to see her at all, her boyfriend, Ron, enrols in the same courses.

After taking the household's reins again, Eliza finds there is nothing else for her to accomplish. She's alone for most of the day. She becomes ill; there are disturbing physical symptoms; she has a minor operation. Soon she begins having panic attacks whenever she's alone in the apartment.

"Immigritis," the European doctor diagnoses. "Typical. It hits after a long period of stress. The moment you feel you can give in, you collapse, because you've already reached shelter. It will go away."

The doctor seems to be right. Over the next few years Eva and Sandy graduate from college; Eva marries Ron; and Sandy gives birth to Clara. By the end of those years Eliza is firmly on her feet. She has started a small business selling knit suits and dresses from her apartment. She carries heavy bags of clothes from the wholesaler, makes appointments with her customers, goes on preparing the traditional full-course meals for her family, and works hard to make her home presentable at all times.

She herself is surprised at her ability as a businesswoman; she's alert to the new fashions, to the demands and whimsies of her customers, and she spares no effort in making a sale. But hard as she works, her real passion is spending; she simply cannot resist buying gifts—big ones, small ones, useful ones, eccentric ones.

She arrives at Ron and Eva's new apartment, an elegant new raincoat in hand. "I simply couldn't pass by without buying you this ... It was on sale and I knew it will be a perfect fit."

She presents Ron with shirts, sweaters, and neckties he will inevitably find the wrong style, the wrong size, or the wrong colour: "I couldn't resist buying this. I thought it would suit you."

In later years, when Leslie and Eliza go away to Florida for their two-week winter vacation, she brings home suitcases filled with gifts for the whole family. The young men smile at her inexhaustible store of gifts:

"Really, what can I do with another necktie from Florida?" Ron asks skeptically, looking at the wild floral patterns so conspicuous in the more restrained climate of Montreal.

But Eliza's real passion is buying gifts for her grandchildren. She, who had been such a disciplined, strict mother, so careful not to spoil her own children, lavishes clothes and toys on her grandchildren. And in spite of her busy schedule, she is delighted to look after them whenever she's asked.

Eliza with Baby Clara, 1959

Eva looks at her parents' pictures with their grandchildren. There are some curious changes when one looks at these pictures next to their passport photos, as if in the first years of their immigration, both Father and Mother have grown younger. There has been a surge of energy, hope, and vitality. In an amazingly short time, Montreal has become home.

The first picture is of baby Clara in her pram. She's making a face, and crouching next to her with a broad grin on his face, Grandfather is playfully offering her a cigar. Eliza in her polka-dot summer dress is beaming down at both of them. Young and flourishing, she could be easily mistaken for the mother, not the grandmother.

Eliza with Baby Dina, 1962

Next is a photo of Eliza with Dina, Sandy's second baby, in her arms. The posture is familiar: Eliza is touching her cheek gently against the baby's soft, fuzzy hair.

Eliza with Baby Robbie, 1964

And then there she is, in the same posture with the third grandchild, Robbie, Eva's baby boy. Standing next to them is Eva's father. Eva's father waited for Robbie's birth outside the delivery room the way he had waited for each of his own children, each of his grandchildren. Then they wheel Eva out with the baby in her arms. Leaning against the doorframe, Eva's

Eliza with her grandson, Robbie, 1964

father is looking at his daughter, looking at the little parcel in her arms—
the newborn. Eva's father is sixty-two, yet his hair has only now started
going grey. Here is the baby boy he has been waiting for all these years.
Slowly he raises his hand in greeting; he tries to talk, he tries to smile at
Eva, but he's unable to utter a word—he is crying.

In the picture the grandparents are looking at the baby. Grandmother's smile is bemused, gentle; Grandfather's is full of pride and
determination:

"Here's my grandson, my Robbie. There'll be an engineer in this family yet."

The baby is looking at the camera with the stoical calm of a young
Buddha.

Eliza with Baby Judy, 1972

Then there's the photo of the youngest grandchild in a stroller, Judy, Eva's
baby daughter. Grandpa, now past seventy, has gone completely grey. He's
standing in readiness for their walk, ready to push the carriage. Eliza is
crouching next to Judy. Trying to make the baby smile, she's holding out
a brand-new toy—a translucent pink rattle.

Eliza and Leslie with Baby Judy, 1972

There's no doubt that the grandchildren are the grandparents' lifeline. When Eva goes away with Ron for a two-week European vacation, her mother and father volunteer to move into their house to look after four-year-old Robbie so he won't have to change his surroundings. When it comes to the children, Eliza's attention and know-how are inexhaustible. She makes sure they don't watch too much television; she plays games with them, has a new creative toy ready each time they come to her house, is tireless in finding appropriate activities at the different stages of their childhood. She even organizes children's parties for them when they're at her place.

All she wants from Eva in exchange is her time. But in her early thirties, Eva has no time to spare. She has to have time for her children, for her teaching, for her graduate studies, and for her painting.

Of course Eliza is proud of her daughter—at least, she used to be proud. But now there is also resentment, as if she begrudged Eva her life outside the family, outside her mother's life. She always wanted her daughters to become professionals, to find their independence, but she herself never quite accomplished all that. She had given all she had to her daughters, and now she feels spent, resentful. And the greater Eliza's resentment, the less Eva is able to share her life with her.

Eliza's resentment at first angers Eva. Then she feels guilty for being angry. She hates feeling guilty more than anything else, so she ends up feeling even deeper anger against the person who made her feel guilty ...

When she sees her mother—which is regularly, and she considers it unfair that Eliza never thinks it's often enough—Eva offers to talk about Ada's sickness, her mother's life, and about Robbie and Judy. But she's keeping whatever life she has away from the family as if it's something she can't share with anyone, even with her mother. Especially not with her mother.

Eva builds walls. Both mother and daughter bump into those walls later. Yet even as a grown woman, Eva feels that her mother must understand that deep down she cannot know every vibration of her soul. However much it hurts, Eliza does not and cannot know everything about her daughter. Though she knows she shouldn't, Eva blames Eliza, as if Eva herself hadn't been the one who burned the bridges between them.

Rob and Judy

How clearly Eva can remember the plea of Eliza in her middle age:

"My daughters have to lead their own lives. But where do I come in? Am I no longer needed? Am I to be left all alone?" Then, the voice of Eliza as an old woman:

"You don't know, dear, what it feels like to be aging. As if the world's slowly grown cold around you."

Photo of the Three Sisters: Sandy, Eva, and Ada, 1961

The next photo Eva pulls from the deep brown envelope is of the three daughters: Sandy, Eva, Ada. Ernie took it during the family's fifth year in Montreal.

How different they are from one another. Sandy with her pitch-black hair, deep-set brown eyes, clear, determined features; Eva with blue eyes, chestnut hair, and shy smile—a different branch of the family. And Ada? A combination of the other two. When she's next to Sandy, you see Father's family; when next to Eva, Mother's family. Yet there is also that mysterious thing, a family resemblance among the three faces, a resemblance that suddenly emerges most unexpectedly from a certain angle, a certain facial expression, a certain gesture. (Eva's "Three Faces" in the mirror—the revolving mirror of years—carries the reflections of the three sisters.)

"Which is your favourite?" her friends sometimes ask Eliza.

"I don't have a favourite," Eliza declares. "I love them all the same."

Is it quite true she has no favourite? Which is the closest to Eliza?

Each is, in her own way.

Ada, the youngest and the most vulnerable, is a favourite simply because of her age. When Ada had her first breakdown in her early twenties, Eva went to her doctor with Eliza. The doctor, a kindly American psychologist in his late thirties, asked Eliza the routine questions:

"Was Ada a difficult birth? Did you suffer much?"

What he is driving at is whether the patient was unwanted, rejected by the mother as a baby.

"No, no," Eliza answers, responding not to his words but to the question's intention. Then she answers it. "It was difficult. Both of us almost died."

The doctor wants to know about the mother–child relationship. The workings of the subconscious, the ensuing behaviour. What Eliza wants to describe is the conditions after the war.

Eliza with her three daughters, 1961

"It was an induced birth. It lasted forty-eight hours. I almost died of it. You see, it was so soon after the war ..."

The doctor's eyes glaze over. He is a psychologist. History is not his department.

Eliza, not quite clear about the thrust of the doctor's questions, wants to explain, to clarify:

"She was the youngest, you see, the most loved, the most spoiled of my three daughters, the favourite of us all ..."

How can she explain the horrible irony of it?

Ada was born to compensate for the losses in the Holocaust. Yet now she is living out the memory of hiding, rushing for shelter, only to learn that she can never find shelter. And her anger, unappeasable anger—the hatred and fear of paranoia—how hard Eliza had always worked to save Sandy and Eva from that paranoia, her little daughters who had lived through the persecution. Yet it is Ada, who was born after the war, whose life has been affected, who seems to be living in constant fear of persecution.

(As a child Eva overheard how Agnes, a beautiful nineteen-year-old in her parents' social circles, went mad and turned on her mother when they were lining up to be deported. Agnes had been a beauty queen, her parents' spoiled darling. When they were being rounded up by the Germans, she flailed out hysterically, screaming at her mother.

"Why did you even *give me birth*? I wish I'd been aborted. Didn't you know enough to have me aborted?"

The grief, the fear that turns back, always turns back to reproach the source of all, the mother. As if the child were saying, "If your love is all-powerful, why didn't you save me?" And in vain the mother replies: "When did I ever tell you I was all-powerful?" And the daughter will answer: "I know you never told me, but you're my mother. I loved you, I believed in you—you were omnipotent."}

Three Faces or Revolving Mirror

Ada's reaction to her sisters during her illness is like lights in a revolving mirror. She resents Sandy for staying away—she identifies her with her mother's indifference. She identifies Eva with Mother's caring. After Eliza's death, Ada's feelings for Eva begin to fluctuate between love and hate, need and resentment, the way they used to fluctuate toward her mother.

If asked, both Ada and Sandy would probably agree that it was Eva who identified most easily with their mother, who was the closest to her and her favourite. Yet all along, wasn't it always Sandy, the daughter who made the strongest effort to break the maternal bond and to assert her independence? She the prodigal daughter who came back only now and then and whose going away, each time, was a new heartbreak. Because deep down, probably Eva was too easy. For Eliza, the battle for Sandy's soul was the real challenge. The first child, the first great love, the focus of her motherhood—through Sandy, Eliza must have hoped to redeem her own abandonment in childhood. On the eldest she lavished all the love she herself had not received during that crucial time, her own early childhood. Yes, Sandy was the true love, the true challenge of Eliza's whole being. She presented Eliza with the challenge of turning her past deprivation, bitterness, defiance, and ambition into something else: into a mother's enormous love for her children.

No wonder that Sandy early on came to realize her power and to use it. The birth of Eva, her younger sister, was the first curtailment of Sandy's power; she was willing to be protective of Eva, and at the same time she was beginning to defy her mother's attempts to exert authority. How strongly did Sandy challenge her mother's authority throughout her childhood. Yet Eva also remembers how strongly Sandy used to stand up for Eliza when she wasn't there.

Eva must have been nine, Sandy eleven. It was a cold winter afternoon. The two girls were on their way home from their gymnastics class, during which Eva had taken a fall. During the class she'd been instructed to run, jump over three children crouching on the floor, then throw a somersault in the air and land on her feet on the padded carpet.

Eva ran, jumped, threw the somersault ... and landed on her chest. She had knocked herself out and was brought around with cold water and gentle slaps on her face.

When Eva was well enough to leave, Sandy took her younger sister by the hand, protectively holding it all the way home. Just before reaching the staircase to their apartment, Sandy stopped to inspect her charge.

"Eva, you still look too pale. You might frighten Mother. Let me bring back the circulation to your face."

Sandy was wearing a pair of coarse, heavy-knit gloves. She began pinching and rubbing Eva's cheeks until she winced in pain.

"You're still a bit too pale here. You don't want to scare Mother, do you?"

But Sandy's concern for her mother seemed to evaporate in her adolescence. How Sandy fought her mother. And when she grew into a young woman, how deeply she dreaded becoming in any way like her mother.

Eliza loved holding big family feasts at the slightest excuse. She never felt too tired to dazzle her guests and her own family with a groaning dinner table. The dining room door would swing open and Eliza would emerge flushed with triumph, staggering under enormous platters with a hecatomb of roasts, chicken, steaks, stews, surrounded by gigantic mounds of home-fried potatoes, rice, vegetables, and several kinds of salads to complete the full spectrum of the colour scheme, the full range of flavours conceivable by the human palate.

Behind the swinging door she would have left behind a chaotic, grease-splattered kitchen with pots and pans spilling over, containers of flour, sugar, and bread crumbs overflowing, drained bottles of oil and vinegar, uncapped soda bottles, all abandoned like victims strewn over a battlefield by a victorious general.

Sandy's kitchen, by contrast, is always impeccably clean, well organized, a shrine. Even if the price—during the first few years of her independence—is not to use the kitchen for cooking at all, or only when absolutely inevitable.

"Hard-boiled eggs, for example," she argues eloquently, "answer our need for protein just as well as the most elaborate, richly dressed cut of meat." With a certain degree of proud defiance, she once served hard-boiled eggs and plain washed lettuce to elderly American relatives who came to visit her for lunch one day. And when it was pointed out to her that the elderly man was used to having something warm for lunch, she cheerfully offered to make tea, then agreed to serve the eggs scrambled instead of hard boiled.

Eliza's closets and drawers were always bursting with clothes; she saved everything she had ever bought or made. In her own home, Sandy insisted on huge closets, beautifully arranged because often virtually empty. In her days of affluence, Eliza had delighted in dressing her two little girls in the most exquisite clothes she could buy, make, or have made for them; in the first few years of her own motherhood, Sandy insisted on dressing her two little girls like little lumberjacks in worn, washed-out, patched-up overalls. Meanwhile all the fancy clothes the children had been receiving from their doting Grandmother accumulated untouched, in a neat pile on the top shelf.

And yet the more Sandy was running away, the more she came to pattern herself on something at the very core of Eliza. In her own youth Eliza also had felt a strong need to break from her own mother; and as a young mother, just like Sandy, she also had an unexplored, unadmitted desire for power, sheer power. Power over the children, power over disease, power over danger. Power to overcome the ghosts of the past, power to stop mourning. Power to give unconditionally—the greatest of all shows of power.

How strongly Sandy worked to be different from her mother. She became a sun worshipper, the worshipper of clearly definable daytime virtues, simply because of her great fear of the moon in her own nature. How Sandy would labour to overpower her own passionate self, until her intensely passionate rationality made people look up with a surprised smile. What was happening here? Surely, Sandy must be joking. Who else would march and make everyone else march toward happiness with the same military precision and grim determination? Who else would insist with the same intensity on inhabiting a landscape that admits absolutely no shade, no shadows, no nighttime brooding?

How strongly, unceasingly, Sandy felt she had to fight her mother in herself. Exactly the way Eliza had fought her own mother, Ethel, in herself. Because it was Ethel who crossed the bridge under enemy fire to carry three crisp rolls to her hungry little daughter; it was Ethel that Eliza wanted to run from when she was an adolescent; it was Ethel that Eliza wanted to make peace with in her recurring dreams in the hospital at the time of her last illness; it was Ethel whose blessing she had been fighting for all along.

Here, next to Eliza's portrait, is also Ethel's portrait, and then the three sisters' portrait. Ethel is there in all of them.

Ethel in spite of Eliza—Ethel *through* Eliza.

How unlike one another the three sisters are in that triple portrait taken in Montreal in 1961. Yet they are also like revolving mirrors of one another. Because each is a reflection of something in Eliza herself. Revolving mirrors—the axis is Eliza.

Even when they're trying to deny her, it is impossible for them to deny her. Yet to become one's own self, a daughter has to journey away from the cradle, away from the lap of the strong mother.

THE HANDBAG

It's Sandy on the phone.

"Hi, Eva. I've just finished cleaning Father's place. Will you be at home? I'm going downtown—I may drop in on the way for half an hour."

"Sure, come right along. How's the cleaning going?"

"It's quite amazing, really. You have no idea the amount of useless old things they've accumulated. That ancient, funny fur coat. Remember the fur coat Mother brought over twenty-five years ago? That was so stiff nobody would wear it? They saved it all these years even though nobody could ever use it. Actually, I thought I might cut it up and use it as a fireplace rug."

"Good idea," Eva agrees. "It would be a shame to throw it out."

"Oh yes, and do you remember Mother's enormous yellow handbag? The one she brought over at the same time?"

"Sure," Eva answers slowly, "the handbag that had all the photos, letters, family papers. Funny, I don't remember it was ... Are you sure about it being yellow?"

"What do you mean am I sure? I just put it outside for the janitor to cart away. It's a real museum piece—it doesn't even look twenty-five, more like forty."

"Don't throw it out. Would you bring it back in, Sandy?" Eva is getting excited. "Whatever you do, don't let it be taken out yet. I want to see it. Can you bring it over with you?"

"You can't be serious. It's old and useless—just one of the hundreds and hundreds of pieces of junk around here. But you know what? I'll let you be the one to throw it out if your heart is so set on it."

Sandy is there in twenty minutes and throws off her new off-white Aquascutum raincoat. She really seems to be in a good mood today.

"Would you like tea or coffee?" Eva asks her after they embrace lightly.

Sandy at that time won't touch anything but health food. She accepts only water. Boiled water.

"Not too hot, not too cold. But no, not quite lukewarm either. Actually, it would be best if I made it." She walks toward the kitchen.

Eva sighs. She's just cleaned the kitchen and the children haven't come home yet. She decides it will be safe enough for Sandy to inspect.

"Go ahead," she says. Then, somewhat guilty about her own excesses, she makes herself an instant Sanka.

The two sisters settle on the wide, comfortable sofa. Before sinking into the deep brown pillows, without looking, Sandy reaches for an album on the coffee table. The big, round coffee table (its legs cut down from their old dining room table) is laden with photo albums from their most recent trip to Paris. But the album Sandy picks up is the new one, the one with the old photographs Eva has just assembled. Sandy begins looking at it while talking, then falls nearly silent.

"You've made another album ... How do you find the time? And what an interesting idea—you mixed it all up, it's not at all in order. Who is this old lady right here next to Grandmother, Mother, and Judy? And what made you mix everything up like this?"

Sandy believes in order. An album is like a record; it should impose order on the past. Control, order, directions for the future. But Eva does not want to impose her own order on chaos. She's waiting for something else—for meaning to emerge from the chaos of the past.

But she knows better than to argue her point with Sandy. "I just thought it was more interesting this way. That old woman is our great-grandmother. I put her next to Grandmother, Mother, me, and my daughter—the family line. Do you see any resemblance?"

Sandy is turning the pages slowly.

"What made you mix it up like this? It isn't very practical to have pictures and letters together with the postcards ... though sometimes it can be an interesting idea."

She slows down to look at the letters, the postcards surrounded by the pictures. Slowly she starts to read them.

Eva refills her Sanka. She is also allowed, without a great deal of persuasion, to refill Sandy's cup with lukewarm water.

The two sisters spend a long afternoon together over the new/old family album. They're comparing notes. The story Sandy remembers is not exactly the story Eva remembers. Yet it's the same story.

Then Judy comes home from school and Sandy remembers that she started out because she had things to do downtown.

"Oh yes, I almost forgot. Clara and George decided to stay in town for the wedding after all. Which means a family wedding. I'm going to look for a place we can rent for the reception. And Judy, I have news for you especially. Clara would like you to be her bridesmaid."

Judy is all excited. Her older cousin is getting married and she can hardly wait for the day of the wedding. She rushes upstairs to phone her best friend with the news.

"And I bet I'll be wearing a long, really long gown, and matching shoes, of course ... Don't be silly. A hat? You must be kidding."

Eva sees Sandy to the car. They embrace lightly, patting each other on the back like cordial business clients. Eva is trying, she is very careful, not to show too much emotion. Not to scare her touchy sister away.

Sandy slides into the car; she's ready to leave. She has always resisted drawn-out leave takings. Only now does Eva remember the handbag. There it is, in the back seat of the car, stored carefully in a big green garbage bag as it's already fated to be thrown out.

Eva asks Sandy to get it out. Sandy reaches back and hands it over.

"Goodbye," Eva says. "I'm glad you dropped in. We should do this more often, really." She waves bye-bye as Sandy drives away.

The breaking away, the guilt, the anger, the resentment. Then the claiming of the bond, the sense of belonging, the surge of being one. These are the waves. Mother and daughter, sister and sister. And the entire movement? The ebb and flow?

Guilt, resentment, and a sense of belonging. Guilt, resentment, and a recognized sense of oneness in spite of it all—*through* it all. Those are the waves. (The recognition and acceptance of the whole journey. Perhaps this acceptance is what we call love. And then the sea of darkness and indifference may become, instead, a sea of love.)

In the front hall, under the light streaming in through the windows cut into the door, Eva removes the handbag from its ugly plastic cover.

The house, the train, the ship that had brought over the family pictures.

It was when Eliza had brought this big bag stuffed with photographs that the family crossed the Atlantic so many years ago. Yet only this

afternoon have Eva and Sandy remembered their crossing. Only today
have they truly crossed the Atlantic.

And so has Mother's old handbag. The huge, heavy handbag of yellow calfskin. The two handles are worn, the zipper works only in short
passages, the corner patches are worn through; the whole bag is hopelessly
out of shape. And of course, as usual, Sandy has been quite right. The
handbag is at least forty years old. It was already old when Mother brought
it more than twenty-five years ago. Because it is the same handbag in
which she had been carrying all their family belongings during those
three months between November 1944 and January 1945. Their three
months' journey between the convent and the ghetto. The source of carrots, sugar, dried peas, the packet of aspirin, and also a small piece of
chocolate. The bag that for three months had been their house, their
ship, their lifeboat, their shelter. Weighed down by her heavy handbag,
Mother had been carrying with her the anchor of her two little girls' existence, the source of their hope for survival, their sense of belonging. The
same handbag Mother chose to house the family pictures so many years
later. The tie, the lifeline with the past, the tie between present and past,
present and future. Mother's oversize handbag, her heavy burden—the
source of her gifts, inexhaustible, never ending—her daughters' lifeline.
The bag with its old-and-new treasure without which Eva could not continue her journey.

Eva begins starts writing in her notebook:
The moment Sandy leaves, I'm eager to get started with my mother's
portrait. To choose between the canvas or the masonite board, to decide
on the foundation, to sort out the paints and the brushes.

I've been searching for my mother's picture in my memory for over
a year ... But the more I search for her, the more I realize that it is myself
I am searching for.

Yet when I find myself, I find my mother also; I find her in myself.

And when I find her, I accept myself, forgive myself.

I forgive myself for surviving my grandfather who was murdered, I
forgive myself for surviving my young cousins who were put to death in
Auschwitz.

I forgive myself for surviving my mother who had covered me with her
body as if reluctant to release her six-year-old into a world of terror, fear,
and hatred. She had carried me safely cradled in her arms, in her lap—
the long, interminably, long years of my gestation—to protect me from
the world.

And as I find myself in my mother's arms as a child, I also find her in my arms at the same time.

I forgive myself.

But do I also forgive others?

Do I forgive the man who murdered Stephen my grandfather, Betty my grandmother? The man who drove my young cousins, my aunts and uncles to Auschwitz? The man who watched me indifferently, ready to shoot me into the river with my mother and my sister? The men who turned my first lesson of the world into a lesson about madness, fear, and hatred? Can I forget? Can I ever stop mourning? Can I forgive?

When presented with the dilemma of forgiveness, a wise man once said:

"The question of forgiveness is a fairly simple one. But you are something of a fool to forgive before you are asked forgiveness."

And how should one stop to mourn?

My loved ones, murdered in your childhood, in your youth, in your middle age, in your old age—how could I stop ever mourning for you?

How should one stop to mourn?

By trying to forget or by trying hard to remember? By keeping a record. Of myself, of all of you I had loved. I remember—therefore I live. I remember—therefore you go on living.

To be a victim is like going through a nightmare. Your limbs are lead, you're paralyzed, helpless, out of control. In my dreams I still become trapped by the faceless forces of enemy powers. In my dreams, almost every month, the Germans still march in to occupy the city. In my dreams I am still running with a child in my arms to find shelter, and when I approach I find that there is no shelter. In my dreams I am still lost among meandering byways and corridors. Looking, hopelessly, for my destination. I've become separated from Mother. I am snipped off her sheltering, protecting body. I am lost. She is lost to me. To be left without her is what being lost means.

Where should the journey lead now? Do I want to continue my journey?

My year-long argument with my husband and my older sister:

Turn away from the past. The year of mourning is over. Try to forget. Turn ahead to the future.

Sandy has been trying to close her eyes to the past. She concentrates on forgetting, with grim determination; with clenched teeth she concentrates on the task of rejoicing.

Ron argues jokingly: "Thank God I don't have a memory. I don't remember much anyhow." He refuses to mourn, but also to rejoice. He is as much afraid of celebrating as he is afraid of crying. He makes fun both of remembering and of rejoicing. He escapes into his sense of humour. Now I see it—now I don't. In his laughter the world disappears: he denies the reality of mourning, and without mourning there can be no rejoicing.

In her youth, after the war, Mother cried out angrily. "Stop mourning! stop mourning! Look at the children. There is reason for rejoicing. You can't go on mourning forever."

All would tell me—gently, impatiently, angrily: "Turn away from the past, turn toward the future."

But how can I let go of the past without losing myself? I can stop mourning only by embracing the past. By making it live inside me.

And what else is there but the past? By the time I finish this sentence, the present has turned into the past. To make peace with the past is to make peace. There is no other way.

To carry on? To forget?

But how can I carry on except by refusing to forget?

How can I stop mourning? Only by not giving up mourning.

By making sure I will not forget.

I want to paint my mother's portrait. To paint a picture to capture her reflection that is not just a fragment—her whole being in time, in all its dimensions. It will have to be a composite portrait, something like a collage, or a series of paintings—I don't quite know yet.

To form the wave of her life, the pulse of her being. Images that emerge, separate, and merge again. Laughter, serenity, sorrow. Her enormous insatiable need to be loved—her enormous insatiable need to be allowed to love. Her courage and strength—her great tenderness. The woman of the sun and the moon.

The first panel. Her laughter.

Eliza is wearing a simple, rust-coloured raincoat. She wears a strong red lipstick and no makeup; her face is radiant; she looks positively glamorous. She is coming home from a parent–teacher meeting, a vital woman in her thirties. The teachers' praise of her daughter is like strong wine to Eliza. She is bubbling over with joy, with laughter. She acts out the discussion, describes the people she met.

"You should see me arrive there—as if I were a queen. Everyone wants to sit next to me, tell me something about my daughter. Of course only fools would allow pride to go to their head. I tell myself: "There is absolutely nothing to be proud of ..." She pantomimes a person exploding with pride, then bursts out laughing. She laughs at herself, at her joy, as if afraid to laugh in pure joy.

The second panel.

The gold-red colours of laughter turn into a serious, sombre panel. There is a bed at the window—a pale reflection of light indicates the level of the deep-red liquid in the medicine bottle, and the level of the fizzy water in the glass on the night table. The subdued light on the silver teaspoon—like a graceful twinkle—acts as a pale bridge between the more robust highlights on the bottle and on the glass. Out of the strained light, Eliza's face emerges, serious and serene, without lipstick, without makeup; the landscape of the face is dominated by the deep, dark pools of her eyes. She is leaning over my pillow—I am ill. Soothing the pillow, she makes the linen feel cool and soft against my feverish face. I know the fever will go away. Everything will be all right. Mother is at my bedside—I let the waves of sleep reach for me, pull me down without resistance.

The third panel. My mother in sorrow.

She and I are going to visit Ada in the hospital after the doctor has told us she may never recover completely. Mother is efficient, cool and collected. Before seeing Ada and her doctor, she has taken her medication, determined not to get ill, not to break down till the visits are over. Then, once we are out of the door, I see her crying on my breast, sobbing like a child and like a helpless old woman.

The fourth panel. Mother is fighting.

But tears of helplessness do not mean that she will ever give up fighting for her youngest daughter. I see her frail and weakened after her operation and long hospitalization. Within a week she will have passed away. She is coming home triumphant from a journey: she has been to see the authorities in person and made sure to get better care for Ada.

The fifth panel. Her smile.

I see her on her last day, an invalid wasted by disease, by pain. She is being wheeled out on her wheelchair from the Emergency Unit, her last visit to the hospital for help. Before reaching the door, she turns back and with an encouraging smile waves bye-bye to a two-year-old boy who is being examined by the doctors. Forgetting his fear of this strange place, the toddler looks up and waves back to the smiling old woman.

These are the sketches, the outlines, the basic colours for each panel. But it is the last one that will frame all the rest. And perhaps it should not be the last, but the central one.

Against a reddish-dark background a burst of light emanates from the right-hand corner. Eliza is at a festive table. Mother was never religious and had no use for piety, yet I see her time and again with a light, transparent scarf around her brown hair, extending her hands to bless the light of the candles on high holidays. It is New Year. With her three daughters she reads a prayer for the New Year.

She did not have a religious upbringing and never learned Hebrew. So she reads with the three of us a simple prayer in our own language. We read it in Budapest; we read it in Montreal; we read it in Toronto. It is a meditation on the passage of time. The ship of the year past has gone by; the ship of the year to come is approaching. We must accept this movement. We must gather ourselves, say farewell to the past year and welcome the new one.

As a child of ten, listening to the prayer, seeing the departing ship against an angry red sky, I still could feel the tearing away of the ship and I could not accept, I had trouble finding peace in the prayer.

My own sense of time as a child was quite different. Before my birthday I would say, "I'll make time stop. If I concentrate hard, time can't slip by me. If I linger on every moment, time won't pass by. I'll make time go slow while I'm waiting for my birthday. I insist on living in the joy of anticipation."

I also said to myself, "I will not, I cannot let my parents die. I will not allow time to take them, ever. And I will not go on living without them."

But Mother faced the possibility of her death early. She told me when I was fourteen: "Believe me, dearest, it really is not so horrible to die. It's the way of nature. Once you're ready, it's a grace. It's not that difficult to accept."

How clearly I remember my reaction to her words, which she meant well. I was horrified. I was angry. She had no right to talk like that. How could she want to dispose of something that was mine?

In the hospital, much later, she told me about an experience after she was brought back to life following her cardiac arrest. An experience she wanted to share.

One day a rabbi visited the hospital ward. Mother beckoned to him, indicating that she wanted to say something. The rabbi paused at her bedside.

"Rabbi, I have seen death. I know what it is. I came back to life because my daughters wanted me to come back, because of their love. I have seen death; I have seen love. I have come back because of ..."

The rabbi did not understand why she had stopped him, what she wanted from him. He checked his list. She did not belong to his congregation. He suggested politely that she ask for the man in charge of her district.

Then a priest visited her ward. Eliza stopped him as well. She wanted to tell him what she felt she had to tell someone. But the priest shook his head. She was not of his parish. Neither the priest nor the rabbi understood the urgency of what she had to say.

What she wanted to say was simply that she wanted to give her blessing. She had seen what there was to see, and she wanted to say a blessing.

How wrong I was when I was waiting for Mother's return after the operation. I heard a woman cursing and feared it was Eliza uttering the curses of the departing. Mother would never have cursed life.

Because even in anger, in resentment, in pain, she never questioned the journey. She blessed each of her children, each of her grandchildren, each the same way yet according to their own. She knew them each for what they were, and she loved them as they were.

As a young mother she had cried out: "Stop mourning! stop mourning!" But she never really stopped living the past, and she also made me live it, made me share it with her. Her joys and pains, her childhood, her adolescence.

And having come to embrace the past, to make it part of the living, she would never deny the journey. To live in the past, to let the past live in you. To accept and to welcome this transformation is to bless the whole journey. The ship of the year past is saying farewell, the ship of the New Year is welcomed to harbour.

I know that to keep on living I have to leave her behind.

I know that to keep on living, I cannot leave her behind.

I heed both voices.

I am my mother's daughter.

I look at the photograph in the family album: a mother of twenty-four with a serene expression, carrying in her arms a two-week-old baby. With the reticence so characteristic of the strongest emotions, she touches her face lightly to that of her baby. The baby looks into the camera with the quizzical expression of the newborn.

Who is that baby in her arms?

When I close my eyes, I see myself coming home from the hospital, carrying my newborn baby in my arms. And in carrying my baby, I am still, somehow, cradled in Mother's arms.

Yet when carrying that baby, I am also carrying Mother in my arms.

My arms cradling the baby are joining the arms of others; my arms, my body, my baby all become part of the bridge.

Judy, Eva's daughter; Eva, Eliza's daughter; Eliza, Ethel's daughter, and Ethel, the daughter of a mother whose first name no one alive today can remember.

The bridge

The photograph of my mother holding me as a baby was taken forty-odd years ago, in 1938. Yet it is only in her death that I have been released to the world, given birth finally, to a world where I have to understand, through my mother's death, that I am also mortal. No longer can she stand between me and death.

Do I want to continue my journey?

Do I want to come to the world of this great darkness, this world where birth must be preceded by death, where love must be preceded by pain, by the guilt of breaking away, where any birth, from now on, will inevitably be followed by death?

When I was a young child, in the vortex of my fear there was a centre of great calmness; yet from that very centre of calmness arose my greatest fear, my fear for Mother's life. That fear has disappeared now. From the vortex of my being that deep fear has vanished. In the core of my being, now there is calm. Beyond the calm, there is calm. The sea around me has turned into a motionless mirror.

There is no fear at the centre of the circle; there is emptiness.

Do I want to continue my journey?

There is a lull, the sea is calm.

For a while it seems there is no answer.

Should I follow Ethel onto the bridge being shelled by enemy forces? And did she go on because she wanted to make sure her daughter was safe on the other side, or because she had no chance to turn back once she started her journey? Or are these two options really the same? Whether or not I want to continue my journey, I was born and I gave birth. How can I then deny it? I have to go on.

I have to find and go onto the bridge.

With a child cradled in my arms, I follow my mother, who in turn is following her own mother.

Am I going backward? Am I going ahead? Going back to the past? Going on to the future?

The bridge does span the sea. And the sea is timeless.

Books in the Life Writing Series
Published by Wilfrid Laurier University Press

Haven't Any News: Ruby's Letters from the Fifties edited by Edna Staebler with an Afterword by Marlene Kadar • 1995 / x + 165 pp. / ISBN 0-88920-248-6

"I Want to Join Your Club": Letters from Rural Children, 1900–1920 edited by Norah L. Lewis with a Preface by Neil Sutherland • 1996 / xii + 250 pp. (30 b & w photos) / ISBN 0-88920-260-5

And Peace Never Came by Elisabeth M. Raab with Historical Notes by Marlene Kadar • 1996 / x + 196 pp. (12 b & w photos, map) / ISBN 0-88920-281-8

Dear Editor and Friends: Letters from Rural Women of the North-West, 1900–1920 edited by Norah L. Lewis • 1998 / xvi + 166 pp. (20 b & w photos) / ISBN 0-88920-287-7

The Surprise of My Life: An Autobiography by Claire Drainie Taylor with a Foreword by Marlene Kadar • 1998 / xii + 268 pp. (8 colour photos and 92 b & w photos) / ISBN 0-88920-302-4

Memoirs from Away: A New Found Land Girlhood by Helen M. Buss / Margaret Clarke • 1998 / xvi + 153 pp. / ISBN 0-88920-350-4

The Life and Letters of Annie Leake Tuttle: Working for the Best by Marilyn Färdig Whiteley • 1999 / xviii + 150 pp. / ISBN 0-88920-330-x

Marian Engel's Notebooks: "Ah, mon cahier, écoute" edited by Christl Verduyn • 1999 / viii + 576 pp. / ISBN 0-88920-333-4 cloth / ISBN 0-88920-349-0 paper

Be Good Sweet Maid: The Trials of Dorothy Joudrie by Audrey Andrews • 1999 / vi + 276 pp. / ISBN 0-88920-334-2

Working in Women's Archives: Researching Women's Private Literature and Archival Documents edited by Helen M. Buss and Marlene Kadar • 2001 / vi + 120 pp. / ISBN 0-88920-341-5

Repossessing the World: Reading Memoirs by Contemporary Women by Helen M. Buss • 2002 / xxvi + 206 pp. / ISBN 0-88920-408-x cloth / ISBN 0-88920-410-1 paper

Chasing the Comet: A Scottish-Canadian Life by Patricia Koretchuk • 2002 / xx + 244 pp. / ISBN 0-88920-407-1

The Queen of Peace Room by Magie Dominic • 2002 / xii + 115 pp. / ISBN 0-88920-417-9

China Diary: The Life of Mary Austin Endicott by Shirley Jane Endicott • 2002 / xvi + 251 pp. / ISBN 0-88920-412-8

The Curtain: Witness and Memory in Wartime Holland by Henry G. Schogt • 2003 / xii + 132 pp. / ISBN 0-88920-396-2

Teaching Places by Audrey J. Whitson • 2003 / xiii + 178 pp. / ISBN 0-88920-425-X

Through the Hitler Line by Laurence F. Wilmot, M.C. • 2003 / xvi + 152 pp. / ISBN 0-88920-448-9

Where I Come From by Vijay Agnew • 2003 / xiv + 298 pp. / ISBN 0-88920-414-4

The Water Lily Pond by Han Z. Li • 2004 / x + 254 pp. / ISBN 0-88920-431-4

The Life Writings of Mary Baker McQuesten: Victorian Matriarch edited by Mary J. Anderson • 2004 / xxii + 338 pp. / ISBN 0-88920-437-3

Seven Eggs Today: The Diaries of Mary Armstrong, 1859 and 1869 edited by Jackson W. Armstrong • 2004 / xvi + 228 pp. / ISBN 0-88920-440-3

Love and War in London: A Woman's Diary 1939–1942 by Olivia Cockett; edited by Robert W. Malcolmson • 2005 / xvi + 208 pp. / ISBN 0-88920-458-6

Incorrigible by Velma Demerson • 2004 / vi + 178 pp. / ISBN 0-88920-444-6

Auto/biography in Canada: Critical Directions edited by Julie Rak • 2005 / viii + 264 pp. / ISBN 0-88920-478-0

Tracing the Autobiographical edited by Marlene Kadar, Linda Warley, Jeanne Perreault, and Susanna Egan • 2005 / viii + 280 pp. / ISBN 0-88920-476-4

Must Write: Edna Staebler's Diaries edited by Christl Verduyn • 2005 / viii + 304 pp. / ISBN 0-88920-481-0

Food That Really Schmecks by Edna Staebler • 2007 / xxiv + 334 pp. / ISBN 978-0-88920-521-5

163256: A Memoir of Resistance by Michael Englishman • 2007 / xvi + 112 pp. (14 b&w photos) / ISBN 978-1-55458-009-5

The Wartime Letters of Leslie and Cecil Frost, 1915–1919 edited by R.B. Fleming • 2007 / xxxvi + 384 pp. (49 b&w photos, 5 maps) / ISBN 978-1-55458-000-2

Johanna Krause Twice Persecuted: Surviving in Nazi Germany and Communist East Germany by Carolyn Gammon and Christiane Hemker • 2007 / x + 170 pp. (58 b&w photos, 2 maps) / ISBN 978-1-55458-006-4

Watermelon Syrup: A Novel by Annie Jacobsen with Jane Finlay-Young and Di Brandt • 2007 / x + 268 pp. / ISBN 978-1-55458-005-7

Becoming My Mother's Daughter: A Story of Survival and Renewal by Erika Gottlieb • 2008 / x + 178 pp. (36 b&w illus., 17 colour) / ISBN 978-1-55458-030-9